Now Is the Time to Wealth-Build

"We each lead two lives. The one we learn with and the one we live with after we learn."
—from the movie *The Natural*

"It takes a long time to learn how to manage money. This book tries to accelerate you through the preliminary 'life' of learning. If you want to make the most out of 'the life you'll live with after you learn,' you must get fulfillment out of your money-making efforts beyond just dollars....This book will show those of you between the ages of eighteen and thirty-eight who earn no less than $16,000 a year how to create your own 'fast track'—your own network of personal wealth and lifetime wealth habits."
—Adriane G. Berg

"Berg states that by exercising common sense, anyone can save enough to provide themselves a comfortable life and retirement. Best of all, the author views money as a means for enjoying life, not as an end in itself. With that in mind, the text focuses on how to weigh various investment alternatives and how to save.... A positive and practical approach to financial security."
—*Booklist* (American Library Association)

YOUR WEALTH-BUILDING YEARS

YOUR WEALTH-BUILDING YEARS

FINANCIAL PLANNING FOR 18- TO 38-YEAR-OLDS
Second Edition

ADRIANE G. BERG

Newmarket Press   New York

Second edition 1990
Copyright © 1986, 1987, 1990 Adriane G. Berg

The publisher gratefully acknowledges permission to reprint text by
Adriane G. Berg from her books Your Kids, Your Money, copyright ©
1985 by Adriane G. Berg, reprinted by permission of the publisher,
Prentice-Hall, Inc., Englewood Cliffs, N.J. 07632; and Moneythink:
Financial Planning Made Easy, copyright © 1982 The Pilgrim Press,
reprinted by permission of the publisher, The Pilgrim Press.

The book published simultaneously in the United States of America
and in Canada.

1 2 3 4 5 6 7 8 9 0

Library of Congress Cataloging-in-Publication Data

Berg, Adriane G. (Adriane Gilda)
    Your wealth-building years : financial planning for 18- to 38-year-
olds / Adriane G. Berg. — 2nd ed.
        p.   cm.
    Includes bibliographical references.
ISBN 1-55704-063-X (paperback)
ISBN 1-55704-070-2 (hardcover)
    1. Finance, Personal. 2. Investments. I. Title.
    HG179.B45   1990
    332.024—dc20   90-5467
                                                        CIP

Quantity Purchases

Companies, professional groups, clubs, and other organizations may
qualify for special terms when ordering quantities of this title. For
information, contact the Special Sales Department, Newmarket Press,
18 East 48th Street, New York, N.Y. 10017. Phone (212) 832-3575.

Manufactured in the United States of America

In honor of Rose (Rosie) Horowitz

Contents

YOUR WEALTH-BUILDING YEARS

Why I Wrote This Book

EVERYONE WANTS to be financially secure. Today everyone can, *provided they start early enough*. This book will show those of you between the ages of eighteen and thirty-eight who earn no less than $16,000 a year how to create your own "fast track"—your own network of personal wealth and lifetime wealth habits. I will teach you how to make money and keep the money you have made in the first twenty years of your adult life—a period I call the *wealth-building years*. There is no substitute and no consolation if one loses this crucial period of earning and growing power. Of course, we all know numerous success stories and many individuals who made their own fast tracks in their forties and fifties and even seventies. But the average individual without a spectacular job, without an inheritance, and without special financial abilities must capitalize on the wealth-building decades of their twenties and thirties.

It is not surprising that most people do not take advantage of these crucial early years, and do not actually begin to invest (use their money to make money) until their forties and beyond. In earlier years people are busy learning to live in an adult world, working for the first time, marrying, perhaps having children. Handling money in a smart way seems to be too much to grasp. Many of you reading this book right now, unschooled in the art of financial planning, are used to spending money obtained from parents and summer jobs. Certainly you have not learned investment habits yet. Perhaps your first taste of work is your first taste of freedom to spend without your parents' approval. Your last objective is to save money or purchase *dull* investment assets. Retirement seems a million years away.

But this book is also for those up to thirty-eight years of age. My older readers are psychologically and experientially in a very different place from those younger. You already have a concept of retirement, you already have been through the job and career mill, you may already have been married and perhaps divorced. You may have children. Financially you are on the cusp: this is your last chance to take advantage of the wealth-building years. However, with the advice in this book you can make up for a decade of financial neglect in only a year or two, and prance into your forties more secure and established than you ever hoped. Planning, not panic, is the key.

You need an antidote to "thirty-year burn-out." This is the time in the early- to mid-thirties that people often feel that their "fast track" has passed them by. It has recently been recognized that adult life crisis comes much earlier than middle age for many. The expectations of the twenties can be dashed when the years between thirty and thirty-five fly by without the expected surge in wealth and security. This needn't happen to you.

For the most part the material in this book spans the entire wealth-building period, from age eighteen to age thirty-eight. Where advice for older and younger readers differs, I will make special note of it. But younger readers should nonetheless pay attention to this additional material. Most young people believe that working hard in their twenties is enough for them to have made it in their thirties. In fact, most people have the opposite experience. They feel *less* wealthy in their thirties. Family, children, a different view of retirement make them realize that the time to build wealth is short. They must then learn good financial planning habits at a very busy and stressful time in life.

This book is designed so that every reader will enter his or her next decade with much more than work experience to show for the last decade. Many will already own a home, have pension plans, have an investment program, and have a good grasp of their budget. Those readers who take full advantage of their wealth-building years will not be categorized by the amount they have earned, the kinds of jobs they have had, whether they have rich parents, or even whether they are single or married. They will have one thing in common: attitude toward wealth. Those who have financial control will emerge with excellent financial planning habits and with a substantial sum that they can build on for the rest of their lives. For them the decade of their thirties will be one of increasing sophistication in investment. They will already understand budgeting, real estate ownership, speculation, and tax savings. Later, in their high earning years, they will use these acquired skills to make impressive strides toward financial gain. When they reach their forties and fifties they will have created their own fast track, one that no national trend, corporate takeover, or other outside force can slow.

Every day in my financial-planning practice and in my seminars I see an increasing number of younger clients and students. I find that they have greater patience than their elders and certainly more than those of my generation at the same age. I find that they are receptive to planning and that they have a sense of accomplishment in following their goals and objectives as well as receiving the rewards.

For those of you who are ready to concentrate on financial goals at this stage of your life, I sincerely hope and expect that this book will change your life.

With many thanks for your expert assistance: Henry Montag, C.F.P., Henry Montag & Associates; Arita Lamarr

Gilliam, office manager, Bochner & Berg; Count Michael de Saint-Arnaud, KtRH, Ph.D.; John Daly, vice president, Salomon Bros.; David J. Nelson, vice president–investments, Prudential-Bache Securities; Ira S. Kallem, CPA, Shine & Co.; Brian A. Pecker, CPA, Shine & Co.; Richard T. Adams, Jr., financial consultant, Merrill Lynch, Pierce, Fenner & Smith; Christopher W. Boutross, account executive, Janney Montgomery Scott, Inc.; Charlotte Sheedy, president, Charlotte Sheedy Literary Agency, Inc.; Randy M. Briedbart, director–financial planning, Fifth Avenue Financial Group; Sue Ginter, Weichert Realtors Co.

Your Wealth-Building Years:
An Introduction

ALTHOUGH MOST AMERICANS have more individual wealth than many kings in history, the average middle-class American feels poor. Our lifestyle is based on what Lewis Lapham calls the "illusion of unlimited wealth," a myth that is made to look real by the pumped-up spending patterns of those around us. If John can buy $300 sneakers, trot off to Zen Tennis Camp in Hawaii, and eat $7 appetizers, why can't we? Of course, the "we" in question may have a child, a mortgage, and a pension while John may rent his home, lease his Porsche, and borrow against his IRA. But his consumption looks more attractive than our equity building, and so we feel poor, particularly if we work in law firms, medical facilities, and brokerage houses side by side with John and his crocodile briefcase.

In The 1990s We're Looking For a New Standard of Self-Worth

Even those who are financially successful and have managed to avoid a debt-ridden, disappearing dollar existence nevertheless feel a profound sense of discontent. Companion to the "illusion of unlimited wealth" is the illusion that such wealth is enough to make happiness; and this promise can be empty indeed. As Lewis Lapham stated in *Money and Class in America*: "Believing that they can buy the future and make time stand still, the faithful fall victim to a nameless and stupefying dread. They possess all the goods and services that a rich society can afford, but because they expect from money more than it can supply they feel themselves deprived."

When self-worth hinges on a highly polished veneer, no amount of money can ever suffice. No one was astonished when in 1985 the *Washingtonian* published an article entitled "Going Broke on $100,000 a Year," or when two years later the *New York Times* published "Feeling Poor on $600,000 a Year." An ever escalating stream of financial need has made our American middle class feel "subjectively deprived."

It's time to find a new, more attainable, and more worthwhile standard of achievement. This book will help you on your path, but only if . . .

You Are Willing to Work for What You Want

There is nothing new about what it takes to make money in the 1990s; it takes a long "hope-line" and hard work. Woody Allen said, "Eighty percent of success is showing up." But the odds that we will show up, keep up hope, and actually take the necessary steps to fulfill our dream are small, unless we get some concrete help. This book is full of charts, questionnaires, and directions. It is a manual for doing the work necessary to get where you're going.

The Most Important Questions to Ask Yourself

If you have concluded that you want to do the work necessary to make money, ask yourself the following questions: What do I mean by rich? Will money alone make me satisfied? If so, how much will satisfy me? Is it important to me how I get the money?

Take these questions seriously. People older than you have forgotten about happiness and confused it with success. Money making is a major *personal* step. It must not hinge on what is happening to the economy at any given moment in time. In fact, there is every indication of a trend back to the go-go years in the 1970s that may make your "illusion of unlimited wealth" possible. Economists postulate the end of a 10-year trend of falling median incomes, beginning in 1984 and ending in 1994. Dreams will become more achievable. So, if you want to make big money, have big dreams.

Now Is the Time to Wealth-Build

> "We each lead two lives. The one
> we learn with and the one we
> live with after we learn."
> —from the movie *The Natural*

It takes a long time to learn how to manage money. This book tries to accelerate you through the preliminary "life" of learning. If you want to make the most out of "the life you'll live with after you learn," you must get fulfillment out of your money-making efforts beyond just dollars. Since the first edition of the book was written, new phenomena have occurred to make it an exciting time to mix wealth-building with personal happiness.

The Role of the Creative Career Movement

There's a new attitude toward work in the 1990s. When you go to see your boss to tell him that you're leaving for a one-man round-the-world expedition, he is likely to envy you, not fire you. When you tell the partner in your major Wall Street law firm that you're leaving for Santa Fe to administer a little theater group, he is likely to throw a party for you, tell you to keep in touch, and invite you to come back.

The Role of the '60s

> "No moment is ever really lost in
> time, it is always there."
> —Kurt Vonnegut, from an inter-
> view in *United Flight Magazine*

Woodstock is a metaphor for a very powerful thing that happened to hundreds of thousands of people who are now between the ages of 35 and 55. If you're a wealth-builder between the ages of 18 and 38, remember that these people are your brokers, your bankers, your bosses, and even your Vice President. These people, the majority of the adult and family-aged middle-class Americans, became fixated on a point in time that was marked not so much by an event but by a concept of the good life, which was not measured by the standards of the past. On the contrary, the more nonconformist the picture of life, the more it was accepted.

The music, the ability to travel abroad cheaply and in packs, and the Vietnam War all served to enhance the illusion that life, dangerous as it may be, was one great adventure. The result was a breed of individualism that stayed in the core of their feelings and thinking as they grew up, had their own families, obtained jobs, and ultimately conformed to lives that were agonizingly close to what their parents wished for them in the first place. Many of the people are your parents and advisers.

In the 1990s their power and majority status will open the door to socially responsible investing, investing in world peace, less debt, more simplicity. The money style of the '90s will grow out of the '60s, not the '80s.

The Self-Actualization Movement

The self-actualization movement of the late '80s is a lineal descendant of the '60s. We are beginning to be concerned, again, about the way America treats its young, abused, poor, and homeless. Volunteerism is on the rise; we each want to light our own personal candle. We seem just now on the verge of laying down our copy of *Town and Country* to pick up an issue of *The Progressive*. When I asked those over 38 what they want to do, the answers were: "Sit and read," "Play with my kids," "Take a walk," "Then I'd volunteer for something," "I would travel," "I would absorb the world instead of its absorbing me."

It is yet unclear whether the self-actualization movement will result in individual empowerment, finding the higher self, and the eventual saving of our planet. It is possible that the movement will degenerate into another merchandising gimmick for the sale of crystals, rune stones, and mantra tapes. It remains to be seen whether we will measure ourselves by the reputation of our shaman, guru, or out-of-body experiences, as we used to measure ourselves by our knowledge of wine, goat cheese, and trips on the Orient Express. Nevertheless, the over-40 generation appears to be a generation tired of "going to its own funeral." Something new is afoot!

But how does this psycho-cultural movement insure that *you* will achieve your dream? It does it by making every dream more acceptable and mainstream. It means that, like this book, there are hundreds of new opportunities to learn how to make a dream come true. University courses, continuing education

courses, government programs and grants, and nonprofit organizations are on the make-your-lifestyle bandwagon. This is all
to the good. Instead of being left to grope in the dark, the new
way toward the dream, whatever it may be, is constantly being
illuminated in detail so that you can find the path.

So as you read further about stocks, bonds, and real estate,
never forget the first principle: KNOW YOUR LIFE GOAL AND MAKE
MONEY NOT FOR ITS OWN SAKE, BUT FOR THE SAKE OF THE GOAL.

1

Your First
Introduction
to Financial Planning

FINANCIAL PLANNING IS THE ART of understanding your own money. Unfortunately, it is an art that is not taught and often never learned. There was a time when it was not thought necessary or even appropriate. You may have had "bank day" in school, when you were asked to bring in $1 a week and open up your own bank account. For many people, this was the beginning and end of their financial education. When inflation shattered the security of the average American family during the 1970s, it became apparent that planning was needed. It took runaway spending and a topsy-turvy economic environment to force Americans to wake up, but wake up we did. We have seen as never before a burgeoning of new types of investments and sophisticated thinking by the so-called average man. Institutions such as banks and brokerage houses are competing actively for the financial fidelity of our citizens. A new and vital industry, financial planning, has grown up with you. All of a sudden, we have so much investment overchoice that our heads are spinning. We've come a long way from basic savings and checking accounts, and the banks' toaster and waffle iron promotions.

Simultaneously with this surge of new investment vehicles and the plethora of financial information has arisen the desire to be on a "fast track." That is, to earn more, spend more, know more, and do it all faster than ever before. The term "fast track" is a real image conjurer. One can just picture a train filled with neatly dressed executive types with attaché cases, gold credit cards, and supercilious smiles. There you are, left behind on the platform, waving good-bye as they zip off on the fast track. A painful image at best. Or maybe you see yourself hopping onto the train, dressed for success, with a network of names in your gold-plated Rolodex. That's great, but can you picture what it's like when the train stops? The problem with the fast track is that it is very difficult to get off without jumping (unless you're the engineer). When you make your *own* fast track, you do it at your own pace, and you do your own financial planning under your own control. You can get off for more than an occasional "stress control weekend." Consider the young executive who hardly lifts his sights above his desktop in the firm belief that he is on the corporate fast track. This works until about age thirty-five, when he realizes that his desktop is a rather low horizon. He may have earned upward of $40,000 a year and have nothing more to show for it than a heavily mortgaged residence, and whatever the company allows. Consider too the young woman who inherits nearly $75,000 from her grandfather and in ten years has nothing of it left, and, in fact, owes $2,400 to a major credit card company. Consider finally the young working couple who, together, earn $150,000 a year and have virtually no investments. Earnings alone are not enough. High salary is an unreliable fast track.

HOW TO FOCUS ON WHAT YOU'RE WORKING FOR AS WELL AS WHAT YOU'RE WORKING AT

> *"It's the story of the tortoise and the hare.*
> *This little story isn't fair.*
> *The bunny kept a runnin'.*
> *But the tortoise was slow comin'.*
> *Yet, the winner was the*
> *tortoise, not the hare."*

What did that turtle have that the rabbit didn't? It was pace! That's what I'd like you to learn. By pacing your savings, your investments, and even your spending, you can have it all. You can have your own fast track.

If you had $10,000 and invested it today at 12 percent, by the time ten years had elapsed you'd have $31,058. By the time 20 years elapsed, you'd have $96,462. Ask anyone older than you, let's say someone age forty to forty-five, if they have accumulated nearly $100,000 for every $10,000 they invested. (They haven't.) Now, I know you might not have that $10,000 right now but, if you could pace yourself to save $100 per month and invest it at the same 12 percent rate, you'd be in nearly as good shape in 10 years and even better shape in 20 years. In fact, you'd have accumulated $23,586 and $96,838, respectively. Not to mention the fact that in forty years, by saving $100 per month, you'd have $1,030,970.

Am I suggesting that your introduction to financial planning should be the old "one dollar a week in the bank" theory replaced by an inflated $100 a month? No. But I do want to stress that *control* of your money is the key to planning. This simple conclusion is drawn from many years of research and hard work. The secret to wealth building is control and time—not high earnings, inheritance, or gifts. It is certainly not luck. Yet those in their twenties and thirties can easily delude themselves into believing that wealth is something that only happens to the other guy, and would happen to them if only they had rich parents . . . a million dollar salary . . . a winning lottery ticket. There's nothing wrong with these advantages. If the people in the forest had had them, it would certainly have shortened their routes to the main path. But if you don't have these kinds of advantages it doesn't mean that you won't get there.

Control, control, control. It's the one thing you need for proper money management. Knowing how much is coming in and how much is going out, from where and to where, is the beginning of control. Some people call it a *cash flow* and *budget*. Call it what you will, it means that you are in charge.

After you have learned where your money enters and exits, you must have control over the money that stays. Sometimes this is called your *net worth* or your *assets*. Setting goals is the only way for you to judge whether your net worth is working for you. If buying a house is your target, having $50,000 worth of family silver that can't be sold is not a good asset. On the other hand, $50,000 of liquid assets in a money market fund will do the trick. Net worth must be understood in the context of what it means to you; it does not exist in a vacuum.

In order to view money as a commodity, something to be bought, sold and borrowed, there are many money myths that you will have to dispel. Even at your early age you have learned enough to help you go wrong. Did your parents teach you to be a spender? A saver? A borrower? Did they commit the cardinal sin and teach you nothing about money whatsoever? Did they seem to know what they were doing but made sure that you were not privy to financial information? I know for sure that you did not learn what you needed to know in school.

The only way for you to "make it" is to know what *it* is. *It* is not a high salary. If wealth building were measured by salary alone things would be easy. Unfortunately, we are taught in school to measure ourselves by a single standard. If you get an "A" on an exam you do well, if you get a "B" you do a little less well. "F" fails. This is not the case in wealth building. If you earn $80,000 a year you have more wealth than your neighbor earning $20,000. Right? Wrong! Those of you who do earn $80,000 a year and barely have enough to open up an IRA marvel at the miraculous ability of your friend or sibling who earns half of your income to invest with apparent ease. Many executives stand in awe of an employee who, after years of earning less, may retire with more than they.

Yes, pace and control require a thorough grasp of your present financial condition, coupled with a hard-nosed analysis of whether you're on the right track to meet your goals. In this complex financial world this will take some time and labor but will pay off as nothing you've ever done before possibly can. Give yourself your own financial consultation by following the procedures outlined ahead.

Determining Your Present Financial Picture

Throughout the remainder of this section you will find data sheets which, when completed, will create a book about your present financial picture. The forms and procedures are a composite of the finest methods used in financial planning today. All who have contributed are heartily acknowledged at the beginning of this book. Often information, particularly on financial goals, is requested more than once. I believe that as you progress through the chapter your thinking will be clarified and you will change or sharpen your goals. The progression will demonstrate this to you.

In filling out the following Income and Expense Statement, you will get a quick picture of your total income as compared to total expenses. The purpose is first to help you focus on your finances, and then to show you how much you can afford to invest, save, or use to repay a loan or, if expenses exceed income, how much spending you must curtail to reverse the situation.

QUICK INCOME AND EXPENSE STATEMENT

From _____ , 19 ___ to _____ , 19 ___

(to cover one year)

INCOME Money you receive.

GROSS SALARY/WAGES $ _____

MINUS DEDUCTIONS
Federal and state income tax,
FICA, etc. −$ _____

TAKE-HOME PAY $ _____

OTHER GROSS SALARY/WAGES IN HOUSEHOLD $ _____

MINUS DEDUCTIONS −$ _____

TAKE-HOME PAY $ _____

COMMISSIONS, TIPS, BONUSES $ _____

NET PROFIT FROM BUSINESS, FARM, TRADE, PROFESSION $ _____

INTEREST OR DIVIDENDS FROM SAVINGS, STOCKS, BONDS, OTHER SECURITIES, NOTES $ _____

NET PROFIT FROM SALE OF ASSETS $ _____

NET PROFIT FROM RENTAL PROPERTY $ _____

INCOME FROM ALIMONY/CHILD SUPPORT $ _____

EXPENSES Money you spend, including self-established savings goals.

RENT Include utility payments if automatically included in rent. $ _____

MORTGAGE PAYMENTS Include property tax and insurance if automatically included in payment. $ _____

OTHER REAL ESTATE Second mortgage, home improvement loan (if secured by home), vacation home, storage rental, homeowners association fees. $ _____

HOUSEHOLD MAINTENANCE/REPAIR Gardening, cleaning house/appliance repairs (material, labor). $ _____

UTILITIES Gas, electricity, heating, fuel, phone, water, cable TV, garbage. $ _____

FOOD Groceries, nonfood items in supermarket bill. $ _____

TRANSPORTATION Car operating expenses (gas, oil, repairs, servicing), parking, public transportation. $ _____

CREDIT/CHARGE ACCOUNTS Payments for charge accounts, credit cards, personal lines of credit. $ _____

INSTALLMENT CONTRACT PAYMENTS Payments made at regular intervals over specific time periods for purchase of vehicle, mobile home, furniture, and so on. $ _____

INSURANCE Real property (fire, liability, theft, etc., if not included in house payment), personal property (home-owners, renters, auto), life, health, other. $ _____

REFUNDS/REBATES $_____

CASH GIFTS $_____

OTHER INCOME

Social Security benefits $_____

Individual Retirement Accounts, Keoghs $_____

Pensions, annuities $_____

Veterans benefits $_____

Unemployment benefits $_____

Disability benefits $_____

Life Insurance benefits $_____

Income from trusts $_____

Royalties/residuals $_____

TOTAL INCOME $_____

TOTAL INCOME
MINUS TOTAL EXPENSES $_____
— $_____

Amount available for additional savings, investments, or debt payment $_____

INCOME TAXES Federal and state taxes due in addition to withholding taxes. $_____

PROPERTY TAXES If not part of house payment. $_____

OTHER TAXES Gift or estate taxes, for example. $_____

PERSONAL MAINTENANCE Clothing, laundry, barber, beauty salon, health and beauty products. $_____

SELF-IMPROVEMENT/EDUCATION Books, magazines, newspapers, seminars, lessons, tuition, room and board away from home. $_____

RECREATION/ENTERTAINMENT Restaurants, movies, sports, vacations, weekends, parties. $_____

SAVINGS Savings accounts, Christmas Clubs, time deposits, U.S. Savings Bonds, and so on. $_____

PERSONAL PROPERTY LEASE PAYMENTS Auto, furniture, equipment $_____

REGULAR PAYMENTS TO OTHERS Alimony, child support, house maintenance. $_____

REGULAR CONTRIBUTIONS Church, charities, other. $_____

DUES Union, club, and other memberships. $_____

CHILD CARE Day care, nursery school, housekeeper, babysitter. $_____

MEDICAL/DENTAL Drugs and treatments not covered by insurance. $_____

TOTAL EXPENSES $_____

PLANNING TO BE RICH
BY

Name: _____

Address: _____

_____

_____

Phone: (Home) _____

(Business) _____

Tax Bracket:* tax year 19— _____

tax year 19— _____

present year _____

Primary Investment/Financial Concern (e.g., paying college loan, saving for children's education): _____

_____

_____

Additional Comments (if any) _____

_____

_____

_____

_____

The forms on pages 19–22 are a quick asset study. They will bring you face to face with your net worth (assets minus liabilities). Don't judge yourself by your net worth, it is meaningful only in comparison to whether it helps you reach your goals.

*See page 213.

INVENTORY OF ASSETS

Cash-Type

Items	No. of Units or Shares	Date Acquired	Amount, Cost, or Other Basis	Fair Market Value	Annual Yield %	Annual Yield $	Collateralized?
Checking Accounts (mo. avg.)							
Savings Accounts							
Money Market Funds							
Treasury Bills and Notes							
Commercial Paper							
Certificates of Deposit							
Life Insurance (Accumulated Cash Surrender Value)							
Other (specify)							
Subtotal							

U.S. Govt., Municipal, Corporate Bonds, and Bond Funds: Issuer, Maturity, Call Dates

Subtotal							

Preferred Stock: Issuer, Maturity, Call Dates

Subtotal							

INVENTORY OF ASSETS (cont.)

Common Stock

Items	No. of Units or Shares	Date Acquired	Amount, Cost, or Other Basis	Fair Market Value	Annual Yield %	Annual Yield $	Collateralized?
Subtotal							

Warrants and Options: Issuer, Expiration Date

Subtotal							

Mutual Funds

Subtotal							

Real Estate

Residence							
Second Home							
Investment Real Estate							
Rental Residential							
Rental Commercial							
Time share							
Other (specify)							
Subtotal							

INVENTORY OF ASSETS (cont.)

Miscellaneous Long-Term Assets

Items	Date Acquired	Amount Cost, or Other Basis	Fair Market Value	Annual Yield %	Annual Yield $	Collateralized?
Annuities						
Vested Pension/Retirement Benefits						
HR-10 Plan (KEOGH)						
Individual Retirement Acct. (IRA)						
Mortgages Owned						
Limited Partnership Units						
Patents, Copyrights, Royalties						
Receivables						
Other (specify)						
Subtotal						

Personal Assets

Household Furnishings						
Automobile(s)						
Recreational Vehicles						
Boats						
Jewelry/Furs						
Collections (art, coins, etc.)						
Other (specify)						
Subtotal						
Total Assets						

INVENTORY OF LIABILITIES

Outstanding Obligations	Name of Creditor	Original Amount	Maximum Credit Available	Present Balance	Monthly/ Annual Repayment	Effective Interest Rate	Maturity Date	Secured Insured
Charge Accounts (stores)								
Charge Accounts (other)								
Credit Cards								
Short-Term Loans								
Personal Notes								
Family Loans								
Stock Margin Loans								
Life Insurance Policy Loans								
Income Tax Liability								
Federal								
State								
Local								
Property Taxes								
Investment Liabilities —limited partnership								
Mortgage(s)								
Liability Judgment								
Family Member Support Obligation(s)								
Child Support								
Alimony								
Other (specify)								

If you had a hard time with the last group of forms, it's probably because you are out of shape financially. To bring you up to par and to learn life-long good habits, you need a filing system.

A personal filing system is the only way to control finances as time goes on. If your filing cabinet is your kitchen drawer you'll lose out on many essential benefits of a good working system. For example, you won't be able to back up your business deductions, you'll never be able to challenge an incorrect bank or brokerage statement, you'll forget the date of your marriage, you'll need tax filing extensions, you'll lose track of the yields and maturity dates of your investments, and you may even be confused as to how much you earn.

You are welcome to devise your own system or to use the MONEYTHINK™ system I employ in my training seminars. Start with a designated cabinet, preferably a real filing cabinet. Use manila file folders with tabs to display the contents. Pretty colors give a boost to this inevitably boring, but entirely necessary, project.

The MONEYTHINK™ Filing System

Each of the following nine categories of documents should have its own file folder, some may require subdivisions within the folder.

1. Unpaid monthly bills where a late charge is incurred.
2. Unpaid monthly bills where cancellation can occur if unpaid.
3. Unpaid monthly bills where some other type of penalty is imposed.
4. All other unpaid monthly bills.
5. Paid bills not useful to document tax deductions (kept from one to three years depending on space and availability of cancelled checks to prove payment).
6. Paid bills useful to document tax deductions (possible subdivisions):

    a) related to business expenses
    b) related to ownership of real property, coop certificate
    c) related to medical expenses
    d) related to child care
    e) related to alimony/maintenance
    f) related to sales tax
    g) related to interest on loans

7. Income statements from outside sources: W2, 1099, K1
8. Monthly asset statements:
    a) bank statements
    b) brokerage
    c) financial planner or money manager
    d) pension
    e) insurance

Plus an updated Quick Asset/Liability and Quick Income/Expense Statement (see pages 16–22).

9. All completed income tax returns—forever—(how many can you have—120?).

Aside from ongoing filing, here is a list of other important documents to keep handy. A designation of "V" means it's okay to keep the document in a vault.

ITEM	LOCATION
1. Birth certificate (V)	_____
2. Social Security card....................	_____
3. Life insurance policies	_____
4. Other insurance policies..............	_____
5. Stocks (keep with broker)	_____
6. Bonds (keep with broker)	_____
7. Notes or mortgages receivable (V)	_____
8. Deeds (recorded)	_____
9. Leases (V)...........................	_____
10. Your will (keep with lawyer)	_____
11. Wills of family members	_____

12. Trust instruments ....———————
13. Pension, profit sharing, other
    retirement plans (V) ....———————
14. Cemetery deeds ....———————
15. Employment contracts (V)...............———————
16. Employee benefit plan statement ....———————
17. Partnership agreements (V) ....———————
18. Closely held corporation buy-sell
    agreement (V) ....———————
19. Divorce decrees or separation
    agreements (V)..........................———————
20. Marriage contracts (V).................———————
21. Marriage certificate (V) ....———————

HOW TO SET YOUR GOALS
AND BECOME QUIETLY RICH

"I understand what rich means," you say, "but why quietly?" "Because," I reply, "if handled correctly, your wealth will sneak up on you." I don't believe in devoting undue time and energy to worrying over money. If other goals are attended, the money will come. In fact, overemphasizing money as an end goal can distort your focus and rob you of the richness of life, so that the riches of life never fully satisfy. Don't do it. Set exhilarating goals, set practical goals, set necessary and noteworthy goals. Let the money come as a consequence of meeting other needs.

When you are young, as you are, goals may seem vague, remote, impossible. They are not. However, some of you may need to structure your goals, and others may need suggestions to spark your own thoughts. By and large, during the wealth-building years the classic goal is investment growth. Your primary investment is in yourself—your education, your business, your chance to write a novel. A close second is investment in real estate—your own home, coop, condominium.

Liquidity (easy access to cash) is important because of the uncertain and changing nature of your needs. Your investments during these years will usually be small, but growing. Investable funds usually come from savings, inheritance, and gifts rather than from the pay-off of other investments. Once your life-style and residential needs are met, you may begin to invest in liquid guaranteed income investments, such as money-market funds, short-term certificates of deposit, and treasury bills, or (if you are in a high tax bracket) tax-exempt money-market funds. Once you have accumulated a three-month cushion (enough to pay all your expenses for three months, should you be out of a job—see your expense sheet, pages 16–17) you can go on to highly appreciating growth investments and/or high-income investments. Which ones? You must choose according to your temperament, available funds, and related goals.

To start focusing on your goals, concentrate on answering the following questions.

Financial Goals and Objectives

On a scale from 0 to 5, circle the number to the right of each of the items below that most accurately reflects your financial concerns. A 5 would signify a priority item and a 0 would indicate that that particular topic has no impact on this planning process.

A. Current financial situation: do you wish to . . .
- Improve your present standard of living?   0 1 2 3 4 5
- Increase your net worth?   0 1 2 3 4 5
- Increase available disposable income?   0 1 2 3 4 5
- Provide a hedge against inflation?   0 1 2 3 4 5
- Provide funds for a significant capital expenditure (i.e., vacation home, school)?   0 1 2 3 4 5

B. If you have dependents—
Education fund: would you rather . . .

- Accumulate the total cash
amount for your children?   0 1 2 3 4 5
- Or provide a set portion of that
amount (i.e., one third or
one half)?   0 1 2 3 4 5

C. Tax reduction/deferral   0 1 2 3 4 5

D. Investment portfolio: which of
these describes your preferences?

- Liquidity   0 1 2 3 4 5
- Safety of principal   0 1 2 3 4 5
- Present income   0 1 2 3 4 5
- Long-term growth   0 1 2 3 4 5
- Tax benefits   0 1 2 3 4 5

E. I would like to invest in my own
business.   0 1 2 3 4 5

F. Retirement income:

- Do you wish to maintain your
present standard of living?   0 1 2 3 4 5
- Do you anticipate a change in
your life-style (i.e., more travel)?   0 1 2 3 4 5
- Do you plan to sell existing as-
sets to fund retirement?   0 1 2 3 4 5

G. If you have dependents—
Protection:

- Do you wish to provide a
guaranteed income in the event
of your death?   0 1 2 3 4 5
- Do you wish to provide a guar-
anteed income in case you be-
come disabled?   0 1 2 3 4 5
- Do you wish to preserve your as-
sets in the event of a disability?   0 1 2 3 4 5

H. Charitable bequests:
- Do you want to provide tax-
favored bequests to the charity
of your choice?   0 1 2 3 4 5
- If so, would you do so now?   0 1 2 3 4 5
- Or would you make such
bequests from your estate?   0 1 2 3 4 5

Rank these priorities in terms of their importance to you and your family. (0 = no importance, 5 = high priority)

Current income _____   Investments _____
Education fund _____   Retirement _____
Taxation _____   Protection _____
Charitable bequests _____

The questions you have just asked yourself come with some modification from New England Mutual Life's "Financial Goals and Objectives" questionnaire. It is this data that the financial planner finds most important in helping the client manage money. Now that you have taken the quick goal test, give it to the other decision-maker in your family, if there is one, and see if your goals are compatible. Where they are not, discuss why you disagree and find solutions by doing the goal exercise below. If you yourself are in conflict regarding goals, it will help if you do the following exercise as well.

GOAL EXERCISE

Part 1

Pick the answer closest to the way you *actually behave or think*. If several answers are appropriate, pick the most appropriate for you. Do not base your answer on what you think is wise or how you would like to act. Then see page 33 for your score.

1. If you win $50 betting on a horse (based on a hot tip you received), you would:
   a) Put the money in your checking account.
   b) Bet the $50 on another horse.
   c) Buy a new shirt or blouse.

2. Same question, but the amount you won is $500:
   a) Put the money in your checking account.
   b) Bet the $500 on another horse.
   c) Buy a winter coat.

3. Same question, but the amount you won is $5,000:
   a) Put the money in your checking account.
   b) Bet the $5,000 on another horse.
   c) Go on a trip.

4. A person should have a will when he or she is:
   a) Thirty years of age.
   b) Has a baby.
   c) Has over $25,000 in assets.

5. You lost $5,000 on stock, you:
   a) Cry.
   b) Tell everyone.
   c) Keep it to yourself.

6. Close your eyes and picture yourself carrying your wallet; it contains:
   a) Under $10 in cash.
   b) At least $25 in cash.
   c) Over $75 in cash.

7. In a restaurant where you are paying the check, you choose:
   a) The special of the day, because soup and dessert are included.
   b) The rack of lamb, because it sounds elegant, even though it is the most expensive.
   c) What you like best.

8. Same question as above, except someone else is paying.

   a) The special of the day, because soup and dessert are included.

   b) The rack of lamb, because it sounds elegant, even though it is the most expensive.

   c) What you like best.

9. You are asked to answer the following question: One train moving at 50 miles per hour going west leaves the depot at 10:00 AM; another train moving at 60 miles per hour going east leaves the depot at 12 noon. At what time will they meet? You:

   a) Enjoy figuring out the answer.

   b) Panic.

   c) Feel bored.

10. Think of the last person you saw before you took this quiz. He or she is:

    a) Richer than you.

    b) Poorer than you.

    c) The same as you.

11. You must invest $100,000 in real estate. You:

    a) Buy a small cabin for $50,000; land for $20,000; and use $30,000 as a down payment on a $75,000 co-op.

    b) Buy land in Canada for $100,000 cash.

    c) Buy a spectacular $300,000 co-op and get a co-op mortgage for $200,000.

12. You have no change for the bus. The driver will accept a dollar bill, however. You:

    a) Get off the bus and go to a drug store and ask for change.

    b) Use the dollar.

    c) Quickly ask a few people for change and if you don't get it use the dollar.

13. You are at a pay phone and you lose the money. You:
    a) Call the operator to get your money back.
    b) Forget it.
    c) Do nothing to get your money back, but feel taken.

14. You get a gift you don't like. You:
    a) Exchange it for something you want.
    b) Use it once when the gift giver is around.
    c) Donate it to charity.

15. You are stopped in the supermarket by two little boys selling raffle tickets for the Little League. You:
    a) Don't buy.
    b) Buy.
    c) Buy only if you don't have to attend the raffle to win.

16. You see a little boy and his friend at a subway station. The friend is persuading the little boy to jump the turnstile and not pay the fare, but the little boy is reluctant and scared. You:
    a) Tell the kids they shouldn't break the law.
    b) Give the little boy a token and make sure he uses it.
    c) Mind your own business.

17. You have a leaky roof. The local handyman has offered to patch your roof "good as new" for $150. A replacement roof of the same design and quality would cost $3,000, guaranteed for three years. A better quality roof of superior design would cost $6,000, guaranteed for seven years. An architect friend said that the superior design would add "thousands" to the value of your home. You:
    a) Pay $3,000 for the same type of roof.
    b) Pay $6,000 for the new design.
    c) Pay the $150 for a patch job.

18. Ten months ago on a "tip" from a friend you purchased 10,000 shares of "penny stock" for a half cent per share,

for a total cost of $50. Today shares are 75 cents each.
You could sell now and make $7,450 profit. However, if
you sell now you might have to pay full tax on the profit,
and the stock is rumored to go as high as $2 per share
($20,000)! Your spouse thinks the stock will go way down
so you should sell now, pay the tax, and go on a great
vacation with the rest. You:

a) Sell.

b) Hold onto it.

c) Sell half and keep half.

19. On a weekend vacation in Las Vegas you've set a limit on
your gambling losses of $100. You played the roulette
wheel with mixed luck and by Sunday you are even for the
weekend. You sit down at the wheel and decide to play
#25. You play #25 for 100 plays and it does not come up.
You have reached your limit. You:

a) Leave the table.

b) Stay at the wheel without gambling just to see how long
it will take for #25 to come up.

c) Keep playing.

20. You're due for a $10,000-a-year raise in salary. Your
boss calls you in and tells you that the company can't
afford the entire raise in salary. Instead he offers a
$3,000 raise *or* a substantial title promotion and a very
prestigious office. With this will also come supervisory
responsibility. You are given a choice of accepting the
promotion without a raise or accepting a $3,000-a-year
raise. You:

a) Take the $3,000.

b) Resign.

c) Take the prestige.

SCORING

Give yourself one point for each of these answers:

1. c	7. a	13. b	19. a
2. c	8. a	14. a	20. a
3. c	9. c	15. c	
4. a	10. a	16. c	
5. a	11. c	17. b	
6. a	12. c	18. a	

Give yourself two points for each of these answers:

1. a	7. c	13. a	19. c
2. a	8. c	14. b	20. c
3. a	9. a	15. a	
4. b	10. b	16. a	
5. b	11. b	17. c	
6. c	12. a	18. b	

Give yourself three points for each of these answers:

1. b	7. b	13. c	19. b
2. b	8. b	14. c	20. b
3. b	9. b	15. b	
4. c	10. c	16. b	
5. c	11. a	17. a	
6. b	12. b	18. c	

If you rate 20–30, you are conservative and would thrive on a deliberate, well-paced, but perhaps slow-growing estate plan, with good tax planning and an eye to the future.

If you rate 31–45, you are a risk taker and would have peace of mind with an innovative financial program, even if there were danger of significant loss.

If you rate 46–60, you are a healthy mix of both the conservative and risk taker and need a diversified program of growth and income.

Part 2

On a simple pad and paper *write* out the following:

The best thing I ever did with my money is ＿＿＿＿＿＿
because ＿＿＿＿＿＿＿.
The worst thing I ever did with my money is ＿＿＿＿＿＿
because ＿＿＿＿＿＿＿.

Part 3

Rewrite your goals:

	Immediate	Next five years	Long term	Date you wish to achieve your goal	How much will you need to reach your goal
In order of priority					

Take another look at the questions on pages 26–32. See if you can find a more spontaneous answer and greater unanimity with your economic partner (your spouse). You should be able to. In the rare case that you cannot, one of you may be laboring under a *money myth*. We'll discuss these in the next section.

MONEY MYTHS AND MONEY TRUTHS

What have you learned that is putting you in danger of being left back financially? Each of us grew up surrounded by a money culture in our home, just like the cultures relating to sex, death, and even food. Our attitudes toward money are admittedly fashioned by our national heritage, our traditions, and our political structure. However, within that grand framework, our private, individual *action* is molded far more by the influence of our parents' teachings. I can always get an audience's attention simply by asking, "Do you want to be like your parents financially?" The answer is not always a blatant "No," but it is never an unequivocal "Yes," either. Your parents are a product of their experience and what was taught to them—in other words, a combination of their historical period and the teachings of your *grandparents*. By the time they have instructed you, economic times, economic systems, values, and needs have changed so dramatically that what might have been valid once has become myth. If you remain stuck partially in your grandparents' time and partially in your parents', you are inevitably doomed.

Now that I have given you this cheery news, let me give you some real encouragement. At the end of this section I will list some "eternal" truths about money—meaning that they will at least hold for *your* lifetime. But the most important money truth of all is that we have absolutely no instincts about money. We have instincts about danger, security, and certainly survival. Our instincts work with respect to friendship, love, and family. But similar responses regarding money do not come naturally; they must be developed. A book that caused a sensation a decade ago, Desmond Morris's *The Naked Ape*, presented strong evidence that man was descended from the apes and that in fact apes have communities, culture, and monogamy. They do *not* have currency, a marketplace, or savings. They certainly do not invest for gain. Financial planning and money management are not instinctive; investing is even less so.

This means that you start out no different from the next guy who doesn't have rich parents. There is no special money-smart gene pool. Even, or perhaps especially, inherited wealth can be squandered or mismanaged to the point of extinction. You have the power to make of money what you will in both quantity and quality.

A word I would like to abolish from the world of investing is "shrewd." People often say, "I wish I were shrewd . . . Aren't they shrewd?"—implying that shrewdness is a trait that some lucky people are born with. Nonsense! In all the years that I have dealt with money and with people who are dealing with money, I have never met anyone who was shrewd. I have met many people who were knowledgeable, understanding, and worldly. When they are faced with a new situation, a different investment from their norm, they begin from square one just like everyone else. The difference between the so-called shrewd operator and the novice is a system of analyzing a potential investment and a knowledge of how it fits into their overall financial picture. They go about the business of investing with a certain style that carries over from one potential investment to the next. Once again, it is not so much the destination that distinguishes the successful investor, but the method of traveling.

For example, no one is born understanding the stock market. Many of my clients, though, are sophisticated stock market investors. One is a woman just sixty years old, for many years dependent upon the decisions of a dashing and dynamic husband. As a widow in her fifties she learned for the first time what the market was really all about for her. She has been successful almost from the beginning. Her success stemmed from three pivotal decisions: first, to use the advice of experts whom she felt comfortable with; second, to check and double-check everything that was suggested; and third, to invest in conservative, high-dividend-paying growth industries.

At this time my client is interested in real estate. Except for her own home, this will be her first venture into this kind of investment. She will be successful. She will repeat her pattern—

she will search for a professional whom she trusts, verify his or her claims, and put her money in the more conservative neighborhoods and the more conservative type of real estate investment. Occasionally she will dream of a foreclosure sale or consider a neighborhood on the fringe. But in the end she will invest in a solid, growing community. She will not make a killing; her approach will be too conservative. But she will be clearly comfortable and clearly successful. As an investor in both stocks and real estate, she will appear to an outsider to be particularly shrewd and diversified. In fact she will have repeated a single investing formula that she can use again and again with coins, tax shelters, motion pictures, antiques, and anything else she might decide to invest in.

So let us replace the wish to be a shrewd investor with the wish to be a *strategic* investor. By the time you finish this book I want you to have chosen a strategy that makes you comfortable. Be truthful with yourself. If you get butterflies about the strategy you have chosen, you have chosen wrong. The only right path is the one that you can enjoy traveling on.

As you devise your strategies you will hit against many myths that will hurl you back to your original starting place. Let me reveal to you the most dangerous misconceptions harbored by people between the ages of eighteen and thirty-eight. By "dangerous," I mean that these are the misconceptions most likely to hold one back from actually accumulating wealth and becoming rich.

Myth #1: People are either rich or poor.

Money, like almost everything else in life, is not that dramatic. People's wealth varies considerably throughout their lifetimes. Fortunes are made, lost, and made again. People can feel "flush" and then needy, sometimes all in the same day. Your stock value may go up and down without your even knowing it during the course of an hour. Many people inherit wealth only to lose it. Creating wealth is not the same as keeping it; and keeping wealth is not the same as preserving it for your heirs.

The danger in believing that people are either rich or poor is that if you feel poor you may believe that you have to achieve it all before you can feel successful. You may believe that wealth is a destination and not a way of traveling. You may give up trying, since it usually takes more than a decade to gain any real financial security or wealth. But if you realize that wealth is incremental, that it grows by degrees, that you can be relatively wealthy because you are wealthier than you were the day before, you will be encouraged.

Myth #2: Wealth is measured by income.

You may already recognize this as a myth. Wealth is measured in many ways, but income is not one of them. Income is a measure of cash flow—the amount that you could spend if you had to in any given period of time. If you are a good financial planner it may incidentally be a measure of your wealth. But every two-paycheck couple in a large city earning a combined income of $50,000 and spending every penny of it knows that they are not wealthy. After ten years of labor, one may have earned a million dollars and yet not even have a pension plan or own their own home.

Wealth is best measured by the degree of economic freedom and independence one has from the need for earned income. It is measured by how much money one has that is itself making money without using the labors of the wealth holder. The myth about the link between wealth and earned income can make the young executive or professional a slave to wages rather than a devotee of investment planning. In the short run, as income rises, this might seem a reasonable emphasis; but in the long run the individual usually begins to complain that he or she has worked hard, made a great income, and has nothing to show for it. What usually follows are job changes to increase income, moonlighting to increase income, and in general running faster and faster to stay in the same place. You must step away from the myth and realize that at *any* income level there is much that can be done to accumulate wealth.

Myth #3: Debt is dangerous.

The notion that debt is dangerous is an enduring myth because it contains an element of truth. There is such a thing as being overextended. If debt is too great then cash flow must be used to pay the debt service (principle and interest). If there is insufficient cash flow to make payments, then foreclosure, lawsuits, bankruptcy, and other distasteful events can occur. But here I am talking about debt incurred frivolously—debt incurred for the purpose of achieving luxuries that the individual cannot really afford. Unfortunately, the legitimate fear of overspending often prevents the individual from accumulating debt for *legitimate* purposes. For example, debt incurred to purchase a stock that is rising (a practice called buying on margin) may be a legitimate method of doing business. Debt incurred to purchase real estate that is appreciating (a mortgage) is a time-honored practice. Taking out equity loans (borrowing against the value of real estate you already own) in order to purchase income-producing real estate, which can be used to pay off the original debt, is downright brilliant. There must be a distinction between dangerous debt and healthy debt. Without well-placed borrowing the average individual is likely never to achieve wealth.

Myth #4: You must be _____ to be rich.

Here's a fill-in-the-blank phrase that many people use to convince themselves they cannot achieve their financial goals. I've already discussed the widespread belief that "you must be shrewd to be rich." The idea that money is made in mysterious ways or by specially gifted wheeler-dealers is a myth that allows you to count yourself out from ever really trying.

Many women believe that money-making is the province of men. "You must be male to be rich." In fact, you can insert any word that sounds right to you. Try it. What came to your mind? Older, male, brilliant, good at numbers? *Whatever you picked, you're wrong.* Try instead, "I can't be rich because I refuse to believe I can." This will come closer to the truth.

Myth #5: Big money is made quickly or not at all.

This myth is one of the most insidious, because it keeps the small investor from taking out a profit when he or she does well. Bernard Baruch, the great financier, attributed his success in the stock market to his strategy of always leaving a little something for the next guy. He sold when he made a profit. He knew that a dollar profit was still a profit, a dollar lost was still a loss. The novice investor, on the other hand, seems always to be looking for a killing. New investors are usually suspicious and overcautious about investing. Yet some of the most extreme schemes can appeal to them. The result is a reluctance to make sound, careful, but slow investments, coupled with an urge to invest in a long shot. The belief that wealth accumulated slowly is not meaningful results in investments in penny stocks, reactions to tipsters, and even gambling. After all, how valuable is a stock that pays a steady dividend of $2 a share as compared with the magic of "buying into" an unknown company that might be a future IBM or Xerox?

The truth is that big money *is* made gradually. I have had the opportunity to review portfolios of people in their seventies and even eighties. Most of those whose wealth has endured earned their money slowly and invested gradually. They reached their stride and their investments began to build on themselves and their wealth multiplied. Very few picked a winning lottery number, bought IBM at a dollar a share, or invested in *Gone With the Wind.* Yes, this happens, but not usually to the beginning investor. More important, when it does happen the wealth is often not kept, because there is no real pattern of financial planning.

Myth #6: The best indicator of wealth is the size and cost of your house and car.

Perhaps in the 1980s I no longer have to expose this as a myth. Perhaps given the cost of houses these days, and the acceptance of every type of alternative housing arrangement from teepee to condo, the measure of wealth is no longer in its external trappings. But for some this myth may hold, and if so, it is dangerous. People of great wealth are often not the most extravagant consumers. The person in bankruptcy often is. Now, there is nothing wrong with luxury; I agree wholeheartedly with Oscar Wilde's statement, "Give me the luxuries of life and I can dispense with the necessities." Nevertheless, spending is not synonymous with having. I'm not so much concerned that you will judge your own wealth by what you have purchased, I'm concerned that you will judge others' wealth that way. In doing so you will choose the wrong role models. You may feel that your colleagues are exceeding you in handling their money because they belong to the country club and have a summer home. Since we rarely know the true state of another's wealth, we may delude ourself into feeling depressed and do very little to plan financially.

Side by side with the money myths you will find money truths. I have packed this book with all that I know to be useful for those between the ages of eighteen and thirty-eight, but there are a few money truths that might not be evident in my discussion of investments, real estate, and other technical aspects of investing. Let me make three principles clear in an attempt to guide you into a money style that will work for you.

Truth #1: Money goes to the proximate.

With money, as with many other things in life, nothing succeeds like proximity. If you are near money you will probably get some. If you work with brokers, give services to the wealthy, involve yourself with real estate, learn who wants to buy and who wants to sell, learn why people want to spend their money and how they spend it, money is likely to flow your way. There are people who always seem to be in the right place at the right time when it comes to money. Those who put themselves in a position to hear about new investments, to discover neighborhoods where real estate is booming, and to learn the economic forces at work will become caught up in the trading of money and the making of wealth.

Truth #2: Proximity to money can be developed.

People who have rich parents have a step up because they are born proximate to money. But proximity can be developed—through reading, keen interest, and unabashed proclamation that you are interested in learning about money, making specific kinds of investments, or acting as a broker or a finder on certain projects. For example, one client of mine is a dentist. He does quite well from an income point of view. However, it was clear to him that his income from dentistry did not meet his expectations. By contrast, he noticed that substantial sums of money were being transferred by young dentists to buy out older colleagues who were retiring from practice. My client made it clear that he would act as a conduit or broker of dental practices in addition to his usual practice of dentistry. For two years nothing spectacular happened. Occasionally a colleague would mention a desire to sell. Months later another colleague would mention a desire to buy. My client continued to proclaim his willingness to bring together the old and the new. Finally, having put himself in proximity to those who were interested in buying and selling (through advertising, speeches at local dental associations, and just plain networking), he engineered three sales within a one-year period. Within five years he had become the most active broker of dental practices in the metropolitan area. These experiences are repeated over and over again. Have you ever learned about a country or a city that you had never heard of before and then found that it was written about everywhere? Somehow, the opening of a crack is often enough. If you can just buy your first piece of income-producing property, finding the second is easier and the third is a breeze.

Truth #3: Time is more precious than money.

I do not mean this in the philosophical sense. I mean it in the financial sense. This particular truth is so important to those between the ages of eighteen and thirty-eight that I have devoted the entire next chapter to your complete understanding of it. Travel on. . . .

2

Time Is Money

IF ALL YOU LEARN from this book is that the time you have to earn, invest, and plan financially is your most important resource, you will be more than a decade ahead of most others. I'll bet you thought you needed money to be wealthy. But money is the end, not the means. In fact, if you waste some of your money I can help you replace it. If you waste your time, there's not a thing I can do for you.

If you are twenty-five years old now, you could retire with well over $1,000,000 by making a single $10,000 investment at a 13 percent yield and leaving it there until age sixty-five. All the financial geniuses in the world can't make that kind of investment appreciate to that extent without time.

It is sad when the value of time is ignored. Most young people today will earn close to $1,000,000 during their lifetimes even if they don't have a fast-track executive job. You don't believe it? Let me dazzle you with numbers. If you earn $625 per week and have a normal work life of forty years beginning at age twenty-five, you will earn $1,200,000. If you earn $1,500 a month, you will earn $720,000. Even someone who earns less than $125 per week (the amount some might spend on two good dinners out) will earn $240,000, almost a quarter of a million dollars, by the time he or she retires.

With all that, Americans fear retirement like the plague. I hardly have a new client who does not envision himself reducing his standard of living at the time of his retirement. Why? Because they have forgotten or never learned the money power of time.

It is a simple matter to begin financial planning early. The psychological barriers to doing this are many, but the practical problems are few. It is certainly difficult to consider the future when the present is so much fun. Money may be a bore, or simply not on your mind. But money management that takes into account the value of time can have most impressive results. This chapter is designed to raise your consciousness regarding the power of time. We'll examine the Rule of 72 (showing how and when money doubles) and also the Rule of 116 (showing how and when money triples).

Examine your own philosophy of money as explored in the exercises in chapter 1. Are you conservative? Are you risk taking? Do you believe life is long or short? Do you see money as something to exchange for goods and services or is it an end unto itself, to be counted and accumulated? In subtle ways you will find that your ability to act quickly and take advantage of the time value of money is bound up with your philosophical view of money. Many new investors do not know how to "take a profit." It may be because they cannot translate the value of the money into the needs of their financial system. Many young people wait until a stock that has appreciated begins to fall drastically before taking their profit. Why? Because at the early stages of their career they cannot see how a small profit will improve their life-style.

Appreciating the time value of money, understanding the kinds of concrete investments that improve over time, and reaching into your own money self emotionally and philosophically will start you on your fast track.

HOW MONEY GROWS

The money value of time can be expressed in many ways. All savvy financial planners—even the United States Government—take time value into consideration. It's particular value shows up most dramatically when retirement planning is taken into account. Let us say you place $1,000 per year into a retirement account and it grows tax free at the rate of 14 percent annually. In ten years you would have contributed $10,000, but your investment would have grown to $22,045 because of the earned income. Five years later, having contributed a total of $15,000, you would have $49,980 (over twice as much in five short years). In twenty years the $20,000 would be worth $103,768!

There are several points to note when considering the money value of time.

- *The effect of lump-sum versus gradual investment.* We have just seen how $1,000 per year for ten years at 14 percent rises to $22,045. At 8 percent the same program would result in $15,645. But what if a single $10,000 lump sum were invested for ten years? The same total $10,000 would be invested but the result would be *$21,589* at 8 percent and *$37,072* at 14 percent. Again, a staggering difference. The moral is that the greater the initial investment over time, the greater the gain even at the same interest rate. Now look how this works with $11,000 for ten years. At 8 percent this is $23,749, at 14 percent this is $43,274 at the period's close. So, if you believe it's just as well to risk the loss of your $1,000 wedding gift, bonus, or lottery jackpot on a penny stock or a horse, consider its powerful effect over time.

- *The timing of any IRA contributions.* Even more impressive in demonstrating the money value of time is the difference it makes as to whether you contribute to your Individual Retirement Account on January 1 of the tax year or December 31 of the *same* year. (An IRA allows you to contribute up to $2,000 a year into a special account where it can grow, tax deferred. The $2,000 itself is deducted from your gross income and is not taxed in the year that it is earned. See Chapter 10 for more about IRAs.)

For example, if you contributed $2,000 per year and received 12.5 percent on your investment, after ten years your IRA would grow at the following significantly different rates, depending on how early in the year you made your contribution:

April 15 of the year following the calendar year	$31,960
December 1 of the calendar year	$33,987
June 1 of the calendar year	$37,190
January 1 of the calendar year	$40,106

Need I say more about the importance of timing, when merely contributing the same amount in the same investment at *different* times can yield a difference of nearly $1,000 per year for ten years!

- *The importance of rate of interest.* The rules of 72 and 116 relate to the amount of interest your invested money earns with the accumulation of wealth over time. The rule of 72 is that money invested at 1 percent will double in 72 years. Just divide the interest rate into 72 to arrive at the number of years it will take you to double your money at that interest rate.

$$72 \div 1\% = 72 \text{ years to double your money}$$
$$72 \div 12\% = 6 \text{ years to double your money}$$

What a difference interest rates make. Not only can you compare interest-producing (income-producing) investments this way, you can also compare growth investments. For example, a stock broker may claim that a new issue will double in one

year. At the same time you may be able to lock into a 12 percent
CD investment for six years. Your money will double in six
years with the CD (guaranteed) or double in one year with
the stock (risky) when you sell and make your profit. The CD
growth will be fully taxable in the year you receive the interest,
the stock growth will be taxable in the year you sell. You can
make an exact comparison of the income-producing aspects of
different investments using the rule of 72; however, there are
other aspects of the investment—such as cost and risk—that
have nothing to do with income. These are discussed later in
the chapter.

The rule of 116 is that money invested at 1 percent will
triple in 116 years. To determine when your money will triple
just divide 116 by the offered interest rate. For example, 116 ÷
12% = 9.7 years to triple.

- *The effect of inflation.* With the passage of time comes
  not only increased wealth, measured by number of dollars, but increased or decreased buying power, dictated
  largely by the percent of inflation applied to the dollar
  over the years. When determining whether an investment
  will work for you in reaching your goals, consider not
  only the number of dollars you will have, but the number
  of dollars you will need given the rate of inflation. You
  will have to use your own judgment regarding the rate to
  apply. As financial planners we have substantial research
  leading us to use 6 percent as the present rate. Will your
  guaranteed interest exceed inflation? Will it exceed inflation after you have deducted taxes? In other words, are
  you really getting richer (gaining more purchasing power),
  or are you just making dollars that will be paid to Uncle
  Sam or spent on the inflated cost of necessities? To
  roughly analyze an income-producing investment, deduct
  6 percent from the interest rate, calculate the accumulated interest, and deduct from that your projected tax
  rate for the year you intend to receive income. For example, compare the following two calculations.

Investment	Calculation
A 10% taxable corporate bond—matures in 5 years, and you will receive income yearly	At 6% inflation, you will earn 4% (10%–6%). If you are in a 28% tax bracket, you will pay 2.8% of the gross (10%) interest to Uncle Sam and end up with the actual result of 4%–2.8% = +1.2% gain after inflation and taxes.
7½% tax-free municipal bond	At 6% inflation you will earn 1.5% not reduced by taxes = 1.5%.

Please note, however—the interest you receive will most likely be compounded quarterly, annually, or the like. Inflation is not compounded. Therefore your actual return on investment will look far better than the above rough calculation. Therefore, this is a method of *comparing*, without the use of a computer or planner, two interest-bearing investments. It does not give you the true after-inflation dollar value of your income-producing investment.

In the next chapter, we'll be looking at the different types of investments in much more detail.

HOW TIME AND INVESTING HELP YOU MEET YOUR GOALS

Most Americans dread retirement planning because they see the future as too remote to control. But quantifying the future can clarify matters and give a sense of security. We have just looked at money in terms of your earning years. Let's now look at money in terms of your spending years. How long will money last?

If you can earn 10 percent on your investment and wish to achieve a $100,000 goal, it will take $14,890 invested every year in a lump sum to reach that goal in five years; $5,704 per year to reach it in ten years; $924.37 per year to reach it in twenty-five years, and only $205.40 per year to reach it in forty years.

If the goal exercises you did in chapter 1 show that you wish to retire in twenty-five years with an asset base of $1,000,000, you need only contribute $2,054 each year to a tax-deferred fund and earn an average of 10 percent per year to reach your goal. Once you've reached it, it will take thirty-six years to use up all the money, if you spend 6 percent per year ($60,000 per year) and invest the remainder of the million at 10 percent. Your financial planner is the expert to see if you wish professional help in calculating.

3

Understanding the Chemistry of Investment

An investment has been defined by many people in many ways. For the purposes of those in their wealth-building years, the most useful definition is the following: An investment is the discretionary use of money to purchase nonconsumables, and entails money that does not have to be used for food, clothing, shelter, and other necessities. When we deal with the ownership of a home, things get a little tricky, mostly because then we are dealing with both an investment and a necessity. You'll get some direction regarding that particular type of investment in a later chapter. But for any other investment you should not be using funds that you need for sustenance.

You are not ready to invest until your necessities can be purchased with excess income *and* you have accumulated three months' cash reserve to purchase necessities should your income drop. If you are in such a high-spending mode that your necessities always exceed or equal your income and you never have any discretionary funds, you'll have to learn the "pay yourself first" budget method (see page 162) before you can even interest yourself in investments.

Note also that the definition requires that investments be

51

purchased. Always think of yourself as *buying* something when you make an investment, even if your investment is in a certificate of deposit or a bank account. Shop around for the best rates and realize that you are spending money when you invest and that you will own something. These expenditures should give you personal satisfaction and should be as motivating as any shopping spree.

Finally, an investment differs from anything else you may buy because it is not a consumable. It is not clothing, food, or any other item that will eventually be disposed of and therefore be without value. This distinction is more important to young investors than they may at first realize. Many things that could be consumables turn into investments. A case of wine that you never open can be a significant investment. Antique clothing that you have inherited but haven't disposed of can be an investment. Furniture that appreciates in value (antiques, for example) can be an investment. As we discuss the various properties of investments, look around to see what you may already own. Most young people who are not born to wealth undervalue their inheritance. I've done it myself by disposing of what I now know to be thousands of dollars' worth of Victorian furniture, lace, and deco jewelry belonging to my family.

GENERAL CHARACTERISTICS OF INVESTMENTS

Investments, like chemicals, have properties by which they can be classified and understood. Like the study of chemistry, in which we chart various characteristics of chemicals to understand how they function, so too investments can best be understood by their individual characteristics.

Unfortunately, there seems to be unending confusion about the selection of investments. Most people come into adulthood confused about, perhaps even ignorant of, the differences between a corporate bond and a municipal bond, a certificate of deposit and a treasury note. At best, we have a vague notion that stocks are ownership of a corporation and are risky. Government bonds are more stable, less exciting, and backed by the federal government or a municipality. Once we have committed ourselves to beginning a Keogh or IRA, we are often stumped as to how to invest the money we are able to save. We may or may not be aware that bank accounts are not enough, that real estate is important but special enough so that it shouldn't be one's only investment. We may not even know the names of the other types of investments, let alone their characteristics.

This section will provide for you the only investment guide that you will ever really need. It categorizes all types of major investments so that you can analyze them at a glance, the way a financial planner or money manager would. Morever, because it explains the different properties associated with each investment, when a new and different investment comes your way you will be able to identify how that investment fits into your overall financial picture. As you become truly adept at understanding how investments work you can structure your own investment program to have properties and characteristics that are most important to you (as we shall see, this is particularly easy to do through the use of real estate).

By understanding how investments work you'll be less likely to stumble and fall head over heels for a hot tip or a quick buck. For example, most people are guilty of having made a foolish investment on "inside information." Most often it is not from a broker or financial professional. It is usually from a friend who heard from another friend who heard it from . . . . Many of these "hot tips" regard emerging growth stocks. However, if the investment had been analyzed the investor would never have plunked down his or her hard-earned money. Why? Because even a successful penny stock is not liquid, is very risky, and imposes a capital gains tax on the appreciation. The potential for high appreciation is generally outweighed by the high risk involved.

Oddly enough, more conservative growth investments, such as mutual funds or a portfolio of higher-priced common stocks, are often looked at suspiciously by the uninitiated investor when suggested by a broker or financial planner. Yet greed seems to motivate the same individual to hurry up and invest when they believe they are getting a "special" deal.

It is my hope that with a grasp of the true nature of investments you will be able to pause and think. You will refrain from making investments that do not fit into your overall portfolio (the investments that you own). At the same time, I heartily encourage you to make decisions. When you feel secure in your knowledge of investments, I hope that you will not refrain from taking action and you will not be one of those who simply sit and wait forever.

Of the many characteristics or properties of investments, certain ones are particularly important to young people. Others will be particularly important to you because of your special situation. As I describe each characteristic of an investment consider how much of a priority it is for you. Rank every investment that is offered to you in accordance with how well it fits with the characteristics that take first place in your lexicon of needs.

The general characteristics to evaluate are:

1. *Cost.* Is the investment cheap or expensive? This is probably the most important consideration for the young investor. Do you need $50,000 to buy a piece of real estate or $50 to open up an ordinary savings account? This is what you consider when you ask yourself whether you can afford an investment in the first place.

2. *Leverage.* To the knowledgeable, leverage is very much related to cost. Leverage means that you have put down less than 100 percent of the cost of an investment. Some part of the cost has been financed. The less actual cash put down, the greater the leverage. Property that is mortgaged is a great example of leveraged investment. You have most likely put down only 10 or 20

percent in cash to purchase the investment, and the rest has been lent to you so that it becomes your own. Of course, this results in debt (which we will call debt service). Later on in Chapter 8 I will try to teach you not to be afraid of healthy debt. In fact, it is only through incurring this debt that you can ever achieve any real wealth. Most of your borrowing is itself tax deductible. More important, most investments simply cost too much for you without borrowing. Even if they didn't you would not wish to put all of your eggs in one basket unless you were "rock" sure of that basket—which would be unlikely in your first stages of investing.

3. *Liquidity.* This is another essential characteristic for young people. How fast can you get your money back if you need it? You may be marrying, having kids, buying a home, or divorcing, and you may need money. Investment situations where you cannot retrieve your capital or where your capital is likely to decrease if you must sell early are illiquid investments. Real estate is one of these, since time to sell is essential. Stock, on the other hand, is liquid because there is a ready market (just call your broker and say "sell"). However, because of the volatility of stocks their liquidity can be a myth, since the stock may be too low to sell with equanimity. Money market funds and savings accounts are totally liquid.

4. *Volatility.* This characteristic is very much associated with risk. Volatility means how much the cost of an investment can vary from year to year. For example, commodities and stocks are very volatile, and within those categories there are varying degrees of volatility. A certificate of deposit (CD), on the other hand, is not volatile at all. For $2,500 you get a $2,500 certificate; volatility zero. Obviously the more volatile the investment the greater the risk and the greater the opportunity for appreciation, and vice versa.

5. *Risk.* Is your investment safe? Put another way, is there an entity in which you believe that has guaranteed the investment you have chosen? The federal government guarantees its own bonds, notes, and bills. The Federal Deposit Insurance Corporation (FDIC) guarantees your bank account up to $100,000. No one guarantees your stocks. A guaranteed investment has a very low risk factor. Nonguaranteed investments have varying safety factors depending on their usual performance.

6. *Income.* This is usually a factor of lesser importance to the new investor. Most young people do not seek income, because they are working. Nevertheless, close attention should be paid to the amount of interest that you can expect from your investment and whether or not it is guaranteed. We have already seen how 1 percent over time can result in thousands of dollars. So, if you are planning to invest for the long term, pay strict attention to income. If your investment dollar is going into growth (you hope), this is less important. Also, with income as with principal there are guaranteed investments and those that are not guaranteed. A CD is an investment that is guaranteed both in its principal and in the amount of interest you expect to receive. A money market fund, however, is guaranteed only with respect to your principal; income fluctuates depending on the market.

7. *Potential for loss.* At a time when interest rates have risen, bonds can show losses, as can mutual funds. Stocks and commodities surely do. On the other hand, savings accounts and guaranteed certificates have no loss potential.

8. *Potential as collateral.* This is one of the most significant factors to the young investor. Can your investment be used to leverage a further, additional purchase? For

example, you can borrow against your equity in real estate to obtain a down payment for a second piece of real estate. Stocks too have potential as collateral. If your stock rises but you do not wish to sell and take out your profits, you can be credited with a portion of the rise that will be applied to the purchase of additional shares of any stock you choose.

Often young people are afraid to invest their money because it will be tied up. However, to the extent that an investment can be used to buy another investment without liquidating, its value is enhanced. Before making any investments be aware of whether funds can be borrowed against it. Borrowing can be done against insurance policies, IRAs, Keoghs, and bond and stock accounts. And many of you know that it is also possible to borrow against passbook loans.

9. *Tax.* As you grow richer the tax consequences of your investments will become increasingly important. If you have too much income, you will want tax-free investments so that you can receive income without sharing with Uncle Sam. If you are in a low tax bracket, you may be happy with taxable income-producing assets. As your tax bracket becomes higher, you will want tax-advantaged investments. Other kinds of investments are tax exempt. For example, Municipal bond income is federal tax exempt. Therefore, in examining the tax properties of your investment look to three separate issues:

a. Taxable or tax-free (exempt)—If the investment is income-producing, will you have to report that income as part of your gross income and if so, to what extent?

b. Deductions—Does your investment not only give you exemption from taxation but actually create deductions for you, so that your taxes are reduced (tax shelters)?

    c. Deferral—Is your investment taxable but tax-deferred, like certain annuities and all Keoghs and IRAs?

10. *Monitoring the investment.* How much work need you do to keep this investment under control? Is it just a matter of depositing money in a bank, or will you have to read stock reports? Some investments require timing, particularly commodities, where you must go in and out of the market at a moment's notice. The more volatile the investment the more important timing is. A stock purchased and forgotten is like a man locked in prison. No matter how healthy he is at first he will eventually wither and die; you've got to look in on him every once in a while to keep him alive.

11. *Inflation.* The factor of inflation and its effect upon investments has changed the thinking of the average investor. We have considered an inflation factor in calculations determining how much money one will need in the future. How well does your investment exceed inflation? If inflation is 6 percent and you have invested at an interest rate of 10 percent you are exceeding inflation by 4 percent.

12. *Appreciation.* Last, but not least, among the considerations. How much do you think you will profit from your investment? Usually, the more risk there is the more potential, but not always. This is where the greed factor comes back to haunt you. A hot tip on the stock market is very risky indeed. There is almost no way to measure the profit potential. It's all in your mind and on the lips of the salesman who's trying to persuade you to take the plunge. On the other hand, a mutual

fund with a track record of five or more years can list its past profits, and a real estate broker can advise you of the appreciation rate of property in a certain area over a five-year period. Profit ultimately can be judged only by its past performance. Dull as it may seem, this is the best way to consider how much risk you want to take. Balance it against the demonstrated past profits of an investment. You may get some surprises. For example, probably the single investment with the greatest past profit performance is in rare coins. Yet many people believe that rare coins are risky mostly because they do not know how to choose or monitor their investment. It is too much work. The fact is that a good planner can direct you to highly respected sources.

The point remains that profit should not be a matter of your hopes and dreams, it should be a matter of what has proven effective in the past. This is the best anyone can do without clairvoyance.

INVESTMENT DIVERSIFICATION

Often the young investor is confused about the importance of diversification. Professionals use the term to mean a portfolio that contains investments with a variety of characteristics. Financial planners look for diversification because investments with various properties act differently under the same market conditions.

For example, a bond has steady income guaranteed for a fixed period of time. A bank account or certificate of deposit does the same, but for a far shorter period. When interest rates rise the value of a bond usually drops, because the interest guaranteed by the bond to the bond holder is usually less than the going rate during rising-interest market conditions. On the other hand, those with short-term certificates of deposit are often thrilled, since their money will soon become liquid and they will be able to take advantage of higher interest rates.

Because market conditions are always volatile, a planner seeks to diversify investments so that at least *some* of your money can take advantage of present market conditions *all* of the time. Naturally, if your investments were all in one place then all of your money could take advantage of present market conditions some of the time.

There is no study that shows whether diversification makes the investor more money over a lifetime. Andrew Mellon, the great financier, suggested that you put all your money in one basket and watch that basket. Many money managers believe that diversification is a namby-pamby way of investing. At best you stay status quo. Those with a risk temperament believe in choosing a particular investment and staying with it through the lean times and then cashing in in a big way.

The same investment strategy preaches that when small money is invested small profits ensue. The result is an emotionally depressed investor who rarely perceives himself as making profits and therefore rarely perceives himself as successful. On the other hand, when significant dollars are invested (significant to the investor), significant profits ensue. If there should be a loss, preaches the nondiversification contingent, walk away and start all over again.

The truth is that most young investors are very conservative. Contrary to the notion that most youngsters are frivolous, risk-taking, and cavalier about money, I have found that because of the desire to own property, the uncertainty of the future, and downright inexperience, most young investors will take the cautious, planned route.

That's just as well for me, because the rapid, risk-taking way of making money cannot be taught. It is a matter of instinct and temperament. Only the planned (but surefire) method of making money can be explained to you. Therefore, for my purposes, I will have to assume that you are interested in diversifying. I will assume that you are interested in modulating your risks. However, I will also assume that as you become more and more comfortable with investing you will understand risk better. You will open your thinking to more exciting investments. You will build up enough of a reserve so that you can take a chance and perhaps take a loss. To do this you must understand the various characteristics of specific investments.

CHARACTERISTICS OF SPECIFIC INVESTMENTS YOU ARE LIKELY TO ENCOUNTER

When you are in the position of actually spending cash (capital) on investments, you will be in the frightening position of having to choose from among them. To help you, I will describe the characteristics of the most well-known investment products and their places in the portfolios of people in their wealth-building years.

Investment Group No. 1: Income Investments

Let's start with a look at income investments—those designed to give you interest on your money without growth or loss of the original investment (principal). You will soon see that *all* of these investments are actually different ways for you to lend money to other people or institutions in return for their paying interest to you. The safety of the principal, time period of the loan *you* are making to others, amount of interest you get, the timely payment of this interest, and tax advantages are the most important variables to this group of investments.

Lending Your Money to Banks

Bank Accounts

A savings account is now considered "old hat" in today's financial picture. Yet everyone, particularly those starting out, should have one. Why? It is surely not for the good interest rates that you will find or for the possible appreciation. In fact, interest rates are probably the lowest taxable interest rates around and appreciation is positively nil. Of course, the investment is low in cost (you can open up a bank account with one dollar) and it is purely risk free (in fact, it is guaranteed by the FDIC).

The reason to open up a savings account is friendship, not finance. You want to become friendly with a bank. Often you will be able to borrow money as a preferred customer and get as much as 1½ percent below the usual lending rate. This is particularly true of savings banks in your area. Of course, if you open an IRA or a Keogh or maintain a business account with the bank, you can usually also maintain preferred customer status. But if none of these things are yet available to you, a simple bank account can help. It is the bank to which you will turn if you want to borrow. Nothing comes from nothing, and a good solid bank account helps you in the early years of establishing credit.

Don't confuse this with an investment—it's more like networking between you and a bank. The properties of an ordinary bank account are not exciting. Volatility and monitoring are low, but interest is taxable and you will earn little. I do suggest that everyone have a minimum of savings equivalent to three months of necessary expenditures. However, I do not believe that this sum should be kept with a savings bank, even though it must be totally liquid. I suggest using a money market fund instead (although interest rates in a money market fund can fluctuate, they are invariably higher than those provided by a savings bank).

Neither type of account is leveraged. For every dollar you put in you have one dollar of investment. On the other hand, both are available as collateral should you wish to use them to borrow. An ordinary savings account is particularly useful as collateral because a "passbook" loan taken out against such an account is usually a low-interest loan. However, you must leave in your passbook at least as much as you have borrowed against it. This turns a liquid investment into an illiquid investment.

The variability of the money market rate might be its greatest asset as compared to a bank account. An ordinary savings account with a fixed rate usually lags behind inflation; if inflation rises, the fixed rate does you no good. In recent years some banks have instituted variable rate savings accounts, which are usually a better deal but are not always available.

Certificates of Deposit (CDs)

CDs are documents (usually a receipt or certificate, not a passbook) that show that you have deposited a specified sum of money in a bank for a specified period of time. Minimum amounts range from $500 (in some banks, less) to $100,000 + "jumbo certificates." Maturity dates range from thirty days to ten years or more. Interest rates roughly approximate those of treasury bills (which we will discuss later in this chapter), but exceed savings bank account rates. The interest is taxable, and there are penalties for withdrawing the funds prior to the maturity date.

CDs are best purchased through your bank with money you can afford to tie up until the maturity date. They can also be purchased from a stockbroker. By and large, a CD will give you the highest taxable interest rate that you will receive for its degree of safety. When shopping for an interest rate, remember that you can bargain and negotiate if you have either a hefty sum to invest ($10,000 ore more) or are a particularly valuable customer. A young person shopping for a bank can obtain an eighth of a point or more over and above the prices listed on the signs in the bank window. Remember too that by law savings banks can pay one quarter of a percent more than commercial banks on a CD.

Many brokerage houses buy huge lots of CDs that have been cashed in by investors before maturity because they needed the money. If interest rates have declined since the CD was issued, these CDs pay higher interest than new ones. Further, they last only until the maturity date, so the duration may be tailored for you. For example, I recently purchased an 11½ percent CD good for six weeks from a broker. The banks were offering 10 percent for thirty days or three months. My purpose was to stash away $25,000 for a trip to England. The money had to be liquid as of the date of the journey, but it could be illiquid for the six-week period prior to it.

Although they are illiquid for the period of the contract, CDs are useful as collateral. For the most part a bank will lend you up to 90 percent of your certificate amount, usually at the same rate as a personal loan.

A CD is moderately difficult to monitor. Making the investment is very easy; however, as the CD matures, you have to make a decision. Do you roll this one over (repurchase a CD for the same amount plus accumulated interest at the prevailing rate), or do you make an investment that has slightly different properties? In other words, decisions are necessary even with certificates of deposit. Lazy investors who merely amass CDs will be sorry. If they buy their CDs with long maturity they will never keep up with inflation, and if they merely roll over short-term CDs they will never gain any appreciation on their capital (profit) and will likely be far behind inflation as well. As their salaries increase, of course, they will be burdened with a taxable income.

Why then buy the CD? Because of the cost factor. As I noted, CDs can be purchased from $500 (although usually $2,500 is necessary) up to any amount. The interest that you receive increases with the amount you are willing to invest. At $100,000 a "jumbo certificate" is available at a very favorable rate, even if your contract of deposit is for a short period of time.

If certain things are unsettled and uncertain, if you have just received money, if you have saved your first five to ten thousand dollars, by all means get a certificate of deposit. If you sold stock successfully or got money from the sale of your first home and await a purchase of your subsequent home, get a certificate of deposit.

Money Market Funds

Money market funds purchased through banks and brokerage houses, have become the standard alternative to savings accounts. They permit the administrator to pool hundreds of thousands of dollars and to give the small investor rates that are competitive with the large investor. For example, a $100,000 or jumbo CD will receive a higher interest rate than a smaller CD. By collecting funds from many small depositors, the administrator of the money market fund can purchase what are virtually "super jumbos," and receive variable interest rates that are always higher than the small investor's bank account rate.

Morever, a money market fund is about as conservative as a bank account, has very little volatility, and is low in cost (often no more than $500). Many companies afford "perks" with the opening of a money market fund. For example, some major brokerage houses offer a VISA or other charge card, check writing privileges, and even lines of credit. There are tax-free money market funds and ones that are tailored for a business rather than an individual. Like an ordinary savings account, they are a momentary sanctuary for money rather than a long-term investment. Remember, principal cannot appreciate and the funds do not boast any government guarantee. Money market funds are totally liquid and are used by many as a substitute for a combined savings and checking account. Like these accounts, money market accounts can be used as collateral to back up personal loans.

Whether you use a money market, a CD, or bank account is a matter of taste, convenience, and interest rates. A bank account will probably be most convenient in terms of its liquidity. A CD is less liquid, even if it is a short-term, thirty-day one, but it may give you the highest rate. A money market fund will be convenient if you find one that you can afford (one that has a low initial contribution), and it will usually give the highest interest rates for its degree of liquidity. For that reason many people have replaced bank accounts with money market funds. There is no problem with this provided you have another nexus with the bank, such as a business account, mortgage, or checking account, that gives you access to a banker.

Lending Your Money to the Government

Municipal Bonds

Municipalities (both state and local governments) must borrow money in order to promote their own projects. To do so, they often issue bonds, which is simply a way of borrowing from the public at a fixed-interest rate. Bonds are backed in a variety of ways. The general obligation bond is backed by all of the revenues collected by the municipality. In other words, you will be safe as long as the municipality itself does not go bankrupt. A project note is backed only by the revenue coming from a particular project that the bond supports.

Bonds serve at least two purposes for the wealth builder: to generate an income stream that can be used to reinvest in mutual funds of common stock, etc. (in other words, to create an equity portfolio), and to augment low starting salaries. If you do decide to get into bonds, become an informed and *active* consumer. Expect commissions to range anywhere from $5 to $20 per bond. After a certain point, most brokers will charge no more than $5 per bond. Don't ask what the commission on a bond is, ask about the "markup." Often there is no technical commission; instead, the firm sells the bond at a markup (profit) above what is paid.

The safety of municipal bonds is proportionate to the financial worthiness of the municipality. Companies like Standard & Poor's and Moody's rate bonds by their safety. The Moody's system uses a, b, and c for three grades of bonds, with *a* representing the best and *c* being a poor choice. The Standard & Poor's system is the same, but with capital letters A, B, and C. Obviously the higher the grade the less loss potential as well as the higher the cost per bond.

Apart from the degree of safety of your investment the question of interest rates is the second most important issue to the young investor. In fact, municipal bonds are a rare investment for the person between the ages of twenty-one and thirty-five. This is so because the two main advantages of municipals are that they are federal tax free (state and city tax free too, provided you purchase a bond in the state or locality of your residence), and they afford income that is steady and discernible, which you will receive on a regular basis until the maturity date of the bond. These features are usually not coveted by the young investor. It is usually the older client at our office who's interested in the relative safety, low volatility, and tax-free nature of the steady income derived from municipal bonds.

The maturity of a bond is another important consideration. The longer the maturity (the date at which you can cash in your bond and the government must pay you your money), the longer your interest rate is locked in. There are pros and cons for long maturities. To the good is the fact that you are guaranteed the interest rate for the duration of your loan to the government (not unlike your guarantee to a bank if you borrow money from them to pay them interest at a fixed rate). On the other hand, if interest rates rise and you can do better with a CD or money market fund, you will be receiving less interest from your bond than you would be from a bank. If you decide to sell, the bond may not be salable at par (the price at which you bought). The cost of most bonds are $1,000 per bond. Some bonds sell for less but they generally do not have the high credit-worthiness that you would want.

Another problem with some municipal bonds is that they can be "called." If they were purchased at a very high interest rate and the government can now borrow money at a lower interest rate, they will "call" or pay you off. This is like a prepayment policy that you may have with the bank if you have borrowed. Therefore, by and large I do not suggest this investment to younger investors unless they are in a very high income tax bracket, need a particular degree of safety, and have inherited or accumulated large sums of money. I do believe that you should not purchase a bond unless you can hold it until maturity. Since most younger people need to get their "hands on the cash" to buy a home, a long maturity bond is usually a mistake.

Treasury bonds and bills

These are a much better investment than municipal bonds for those in their wealth-building years. Treasury bonds are bonds issued by the United States government rather than by municipalities. They are state and city tax free, but they are not federally tax free. If you are wondering why municipal bonds are federal tax free and treasury (also called federal or government) bonds are state tax free, you missed your history lesson at some point. The Constitution prohibits the federal government from taxing the state and the state the federal.

Our greatest income tax is imposed by the federal government. Therefore municipal bonds favor those who want to save federal taxes because they are in a high bracket, and treasury bonds favor the younger person who is still in a low tax bracket. Federal bonds are only partially tax free (state and city). The larger portion of tax will still be paid and therefore the bond usually pays a higher interest rate than a municipal. Treasury bonds and bills of course have the extra added attraction that they are backed by the credit worthiness of the United States government rather than by the municipalities.

These government securities vary considerably in cost and maturity. Most young investors (and older ones too) are confused about the variety. Here is a list that I hope will straighten things out:

- Treasury bonds: Maturities of 10, 20, and 25 years. Cost—$1,000 per bond.

- Treasury notes: Varying maturities, issued for shorter terms than bonds. Cost—$1,000 or more.
- Treasury bills: Maturities of 13 to 26 weeks. Cost—$10,000 for the first purchase and $5,000 for multiples.
- Treasury notes: Maturities of 52 weeks up to 10 years. Cost—$5,000, although denominations of $1,000 can be available.
- Agency bonds and notes (such as GNMAs—Government National Mortgage Association): Maturities of 30 years. Cost—$25,000 for the popular GNMAs. These are issued by a governmental agency, not by the federal government itself, and therefore they are taxed by the state and municipalities.
- Savings bonds EE and HH: Varying maturities. Cost—$50 to $10,000. (Leave these for gifts if you can't think of anything better to buy.)

The younger person seeking income is best off choosing a US note or bond rather than a municipal bond. Interest rates are taxable, but they are also higher, particularly in the case of a treasury bill with 13 or 26 weeks duration. You have a very liquid, short-term investment. As with CDs, which are geared to the interest rates paid by treasury bills, you do have to monitor your investment. Because they come due so quickly you have to know what you want to do next. In fact, a CD stacks up favorably to a treasury bill only if you are really interested in keeping the rate locked in for more than a 13- or 26-week period.

The most important property of bills, notes, and bonds is that they are income-producing assets. They do not appreciate unless interest rates go down tremendously and you wish to sell the issue above par.

Treasury bills and bonds can be leveraged. They may be purchased with as little as 10 percent down. However, their value does not rise with inflation (there is no inflation protection). If you believe inflationary times are ahead, don't buy.

Lending Money to Corporations

Corporate Bonds

Like stock, corporate bonds are a way of investing in corporations. However, instead of owning some of the equity (value) of the corporation, one lends money to the corporation and is paid back at a fixed amount. The quality of corporate bonds is much like that of municipal bonds; it all depends on the credit-worthiness of the corporation that you deal with. Most corporate bonds are issued in $1,000 denominations and are not a difficult investment to make from a cost point of view. However, the income is taxable, making it a good investment for IRAs and Keoghs (see Chapter 10), but a poor investment for the wealth builder with a high salary.

Corporate bondholders usually earn more interest than government bondholders. However, there is no government guarantee or FDIC insurance. Occasionally a company can go bankrupt, and in that case, you are a secured creditor in bankruptcy. While the interest rates on corporate bonds are high there may be a call factor. This means that the bond can be prepaid before its maturity date. This is significant if the bond was purchased in order to lock in high income over a long period of time. If the bond can be called by a certain date, you are really locking in that income only until the call date, not until the maturity date.

Two new types of corporate bonds have been issued recently and have proved very popular. Many municipal bonds have followed suit with the same types. These bonds are the discount bond and the zero coupon bond.

A discount bond is one that is sold way below the par value (face value). Therefore, when the bond matures, you will receive more than you paid for the bond. Why is the corporation so good to you? Because interest rates on these bonds are usually low. To make up for this they are sold at a discount. Again, this is a good kind of bond to buy if the company is very credit-worthy and if you are not in need of immediate income to live on.

Zero coupon bonds have no interest income at all; you receive only the appreciation (the difference between what you paid for the bond and its maturity price). Since there is no interim income forthcoming, these types of bonds are usually bought for your IRA, Keogh, or other plan in which you are not expecting to receive cash flow from your investment. It is important to remember that the increased value of your security is ordinary income, not capital gain. It's even more important to be aware of what I call "fictitious income"—income that you receive on paper each year (although not in your pocket) because your bond has appreciated in value. You will be paying taxes on this unreceived income on a yearly basis in the year that it is credited to the bond. Because of this, I once again suggest zero coupon bonds for your IRAs and Keoghs. It will be taxable (but you don't care, the plan is tax deferred), and you will get high interest and a predictable maturity amount.

As the general public continues to watch interest rates like a hawk, and interest rates remain volatile, watch out for the possibility of varying rates in corporate bonds. It is usually a good idea to take advantage of these unless you have been lucky enough to hit a corporate bond at the peak of the market and lock in the interest.

Corporate bonds are excellent collateral and can be bought on margin, with you putting only 10 percent down. They have no inflation protection, but they are considered a safe and steady source of income. To combat the lack of inflation protection, some bonds are backed by gold and silver. This simply means that you may redeem them either in currency at their face value or at a specific amount of hard metal. If ten ounces of gold or silver back your bond then you can opt to receive ten ounces at the date of maturity. If inflation is rampant that ten ounces might be worth more than the cash. If inflation is low then you will take the currency instead. You've learned by now that you get nothing for nothing. Usually this desirable inflation protection is accompanied by a much lower interest rate.

Tips about Interest-Bearing Investments

1. Long-term interest rates are less volatile than short-term rates. Always remember that you need not rush into a long-term loan investment; you'll get just about the same interest rate if you buy it a month or two later.

2. Short-term interest rates are generally lower than long-term rates, but they leave your investment more liquid. They are also more volatile.

3. Tax-exempt bonds have the lowest rates, so invest in these only if you are in a high tax bracket.

4. Treasury bonds do less well than industrial (corporate bonds), but are state tax free.

5. By and large home mortgages, the cost of your borrowing money, are always greater than what you get as interest when you lend money. This is a hint for you to look at my chapter on real estate, which teaches you how to lend your money to others for their home mortgages (Chapter 6).

6. A private investment account for over $200,000 gives the highest short-term rates. This shows why money markets, which have lots of pooled money to invest, can do better than small individual bank accounts.

Investment Group No. 2: Growth Investments

Most wealth builders will prefer to invest for growth rather than simply increase income. Perhaps the finest such wealth-building investment is real estate, to which Chapter 6 is devoted. But there are certainly others. Just because an investment doesn't pay interest doesn't mean it's a good growth investment. Remember too that some growth investments do give income, in the form of dividends. In choosing an investment for growth, remember the Rule of 72: the average nongrowth, guaranteed-principal investment doubles in no more than seven years. If you can't expect at least that much growth, don't bother with that particular investment. Steady interest can outstrip growth.

Stocks

The ownership of common stock is probably the most difficult investment for the new investor. Yet it is what many novices consider the only "true" investment. When you own common stock, you own a share in a corporation—an interest in a company over which you have no management and no control except a shareholder's vote. You are entitled to dividends (distribution of excess profits, if any) and, most important, you have a ready market for your shares should you wish to sell them. Stocks are actually quite liquid because there is an instantaneous market (the stock exchanges) that permits you to sell at a moment's notice. However, they do not get high marks overall for liquidity because they cannot be liquidated at a controlled price.

Stocks are also difficult to monitor and should not be considered as an investment unless they are also considered an important hobby. If you enjoy analysis, reading about stocks, and following yearly financial statements of the companies in which you invest, you will probably be successful in buying stocks. I have found them the most difficult investment to teach, however.

The lure of stocks is the potential for appreciation. If a company does well you will make money. Moreover, that money will not be fully taxed, but will be taxed as a capital gain—you'll be taxed only on 40 percent of what you've earned (see page 215). Your gains can even be offset by any losses you might have incurred, thus reducing your taxes further. And if you buy a sufficient amount of dividend-paying stock, you have income as well as appreciation—a combination you get with very few investments.

The key to dealing with stocks is to know that their properties vary. When selecting a stock use the same criteria that you would in comparing investments with one another. For example, some stocks are dividend-producing and therefore yield income. Some have only long-term appreciation, yielding no income whatsoever. Some stocks (those of new companies, new and growing industries, industries in a blight, companies with new management) are very volatile; others (old, established companies with a long-unchanging mode of operation, sometimes called "blue chip" companies) stay relatively steady. Investors who want to take chances, keep an eye on their investments, and perhaps make a killing favor the first type. Investors who want dividends, even from common stock, and are interested in steady principal without headaches favor the latter. Timing and the need to monitor the progress of stocks vary widely with the stock purchased.

When selecting stocks you will naturally consider costs. First of all, remember that you pay a commission to your broker or dealer when you buy and sell your shares of stock, which must always be calculated in determining whether you've actually made a profit. Some stocks cost more than $100 per share, while others can literally be purchased for a penny. In general, stocks are purchased at 100 shares per lot. However, an odd lot (less than 100 shares) can be purchased either through a broker, who will generally charge an additional commission, or through an odd lot dealer. It is suggested that you save the extra commission and try to purchase a round lot.

As already discussed, the properties of leverage and risk can be partially controlled by the investor. Fifty percent of your stock purchase can be made "on margin"—that is, the broker-dealer will lend you half of the money you require for investment at an appropriate interest rate. Not all stocks can be purchased on margin. If the value of your stock dips below a certain amount you will receive a margin call, where you are asked to tender enough money to balance your account. On the other hand, if your stock rises above a certain dollar value the brokerage house will open a supplemental margin account and credit you with dollars that you can use to buy additional stock. Risks can also be partially controlled by your placing certain instructions with your broker. For example, a stop order will instruct your broker to sell stock if it dips under a certain price. Young investors are usually ignorant or confused with regard to these instructions. You don't have to let a stock go down indefinitely. Most stock analysts will tell you that the greatest problem with new investors is their fear of selling, not their fear of buying. If you see a profit, take it; if you are concerned about a loss, sell and get clear. To control your investment use the following instructions freely:

Day order—An order to buy or sell which, if not executed, expires at the end of the trading day on which it was entered.

Good 'til cancelled order (GTC) or open order—An order to buy or sell that remains in effect until it is either executed or cancelled.

Limit order, limited order, or limited price order—An order to buy or sell a stated amount of a security at a specified price, or at a better price if obtainable, after the order is represented to the traders.

Market order—An order to buy or sell a stated amount of a security at the most advantageous price obtainable after the order is represented on the trading floor (see: good 'til cancelled order, limit order, stop order).

Stop order—An order to buy at a price above or sell at a price below the current market. *Stop buy orders* are generally used to limit loss or protect unrealized profits on a short sale. *Stop sell orders* are generally used to protect unrealized profits or limit loss on a holding. A stop order becomes a market order when the stock sells at or above the specified price and, thus, may not necessarily be executed at that price.

Stop limit order—A stop order that becomes a limit order after the specified stop price has been reached (see: limit order, stop order).

An interesting newsletter for the new investor is the *Bowser Report* (P.O. Box 6278, Newport News, VA 23606). Basically Bowser deals only with stock selling for $3 per share. He grades the stock by various criteria and when they fall below the criteria he suggests a sell. The point of the system is that it *is* a system. It keeps you in touch and connected with the stocks you have chosen. A good broker can do the same. If you are a purely passive investor I don't suggest purchasing stock. If you are serious about it, invest serious money and be serious about planning your portfolio. *Valueline* is another good tool for keeping abreast of stocks and their particular properties (their address is 711 3rd Avenue, New York, N.Y. 10017). If you do become savvy enough to place your own orders, you should use a discount broker who will not give you suggestions or service but will charge you far less of a commission than a retail broker. *The Wall Street Journal* and *Barron's* contain advertising for such brokers.

It is not wise just to listen passively to a broker. It's not that they are salesmen who are there to lead you astray—on the contrary, securities brokers usually believe in what they have to sell and often invest themselves in the things that they are suggesting to their clients. There are two reasons why you shouldn't rely solely on a broker. First, no broker can analyze every issue or every stock. Even in the largest brokerage houses there are specialists. Therefore, a broker may not be concentrating on the industries or types of stocks with which you are comfortable. If you rely solely on a broker you will be waiting for him or her to call you with a suggestion that may come at a time when you are not ready to make an additional investment, or may come too late, after you have already invested your funds. You must let your broker know when you are ready to invest and maintain a continuous dialogue with him or her.

The second, more important, reason that relying on a broker is a problem is that brokers are not financial planners. They do not have the entire picture of your finances. They may not know that you need tax-free income, or liquidity at a certain time, or that you are hoping to take a loss because you have just sold a piece of real estate for a gain. Although many brokers present themselves as financial planners, they usually do not offer an in-depth service. True financial planning is very time consuming and can be far too expensive for a broker to engage in without payment. Once again, you must be in good control of all your finances so that you can work with a broker as the unique professional he or she is.

The income factor can be partially controlled by the investor in stocks. The following are definitions of various types of stock that more or less meet income as a goal:

- *Preferred stock*—The owner of preferred stock will receive its income (dividend) before a shareholder of common stock. Preferred stock is not issued by every corporation and is therefore not available to the investor for every company in which he or she wishes to invest. A stockbroker should be consulted to learn which companies issue preferred shares and what their track records have been. It is the stockbroker's favorite companies that you will learn about, but for those selected companies you will get a thorough printout of past performance, dividend history, and other significant information.

- *Cumulative preferred stock*—In any year that a dividend is not declared, the holder of cumulative preferred stock will still be entitled to receive that dividend in the future when and if a dividend is declared. In other words, the missing dividends will accumulate and eventually be paid.

- *Cumulative convertible preferred stock*—With such a stock you can convert your preferred shares into common stock.

The properties of these types of stock are essentially the same as common stock, except that they are relatively less volatile and generally do not appreciate or depreciate to the same extent. There is also more safety for income production.

On the down side, a share of preferred stock is more expensive than a share of common stock in the same corporation—but this can be an advantage if your preferred stock can be converted into common stock. When preferred stock is purchased there is an agreement that the shareholder can convert the stock at a fixed dollar amount per share of common stock. For example, at $200 a share for a preferred stock an agreement would be made at the time of purchase that said shares could be converted into ten shares of common stock. Perhaps at that time each share of common stock was evaluated at $10 per share. If the common stock rises to $25 a share the conversion is still ten shares, resulting in a profit of $5 per share if the shareholder converts and then sells.

Sometimes preferred shares themselves will rise and they can be sold at the same profit. Preferred shares can also be redeemed by the corporation at full market price. This sometimes happens when the value of the common stock rises considerably, to avoid mass conversion of preferred shares into the more valuable common shares; check on the price at which a preferred share can be redeemed.

In brief, most of these types of stock are inappropriate for the new investor. Preferred stock (noncumulative) does very little for you. If a dividend is not declared, you miss it—it's gone forever. The price per share is always higher than that of a common stock and the volatility is no different. There is not much greater value in cumulative preferred stock. The reason that these types of stock are of interest is that 85 percent of the dividend is tax exempt if the stock is owned by a corporation. Uncle Sam wants to encourage companies to invest in other companies. As time goes on and if you become very sophisticated, you may want to form a corporation whose purpose is to invest in other corporations (own stocks) to get the advantage of this tax exemption. You may already have a corporation as part of your own business. If so, consider investing at least some of your capital in dividend-paying stock rather than money market funds or other more "safe" investments, because of the excellent tax advantages given to corporate purchasers of preferred shares.

Finally, preferred stocks are useful for those of you interested in income. Except for the convertible shares, these shares do not participate in a rising market or in the appreciation or profits of the company. Instead, they guarantee income. Of course, if the company goes bust they are not insured, unlike other income-producing investments such as money markets, CDs, and bank accounts. Their value or price fluctuates with interest rates, not with the market value of the common stock of the underlying corporation. If interest rates are high, preferred shares will be expensive, but worth it. You will be locking in high yields. If you expect interest rates to drop you may view the cumulative preferred shares with admiration. Remember, however, that this is a sophisticated investment because you must be able to deduce two factors: the eventual lowering of interest rates, and the eventual profitability of a corporation (so that dividends will be paid in the first place).

Options

The reason for buying a stock option (the right to purchase stock at a given price) is your belief that the stock's price is going up. In a hypothetical example, you have noticed that the management of Amerada Hess is improving. The stock is selling for $24 per share. You buy an option to buy 100 shares, for the usual cost of about $2 per share, giving you the right to actually purchase the shares for $30 apiece within the next nine months. You wait and see. If Amerada Hess doesn't increase, you don't buy—you lost $200 (100 shares × $2). If it increases over $32, you buy at $30 per share and resell immediately. Let's say it's up to $36. You made $4 a share—$30 paid plus $2 for the option equals $32 paid, and $36 sold equals $4 profit. On 100 shares you make $400 by investing $200—a profit of 100 percent. This is called *buying a call*.

You can also sell a call. If you already own Amerada Hess

and you *don't* think it will go up appreciably, sell the option to buy at $30 for $2 per share. If the option runs out and is never exercised, you earned $200 for every 100 shares by doing nothing but *selling* the call option. Naturally, if the stock goes up it will be "called away"—the person who bought the option will now buy the stock. You'll get $30 plus $2, or $32 per share. If you bought lower you will still make a profit. If you sell many calls through the years then you will enjoy added gains from a stock that may never actually rise in value. Such gain is always a *short-term* capital gain.

A dangerous thing to do is to write (sell) "naked" options— selling the option to buy without owning the stock. This is trying to make something for nothing. Forget it. If the stock goes up and the stock is called, you'll have to buy it at the high price and resell at the lower option price.

Perhaps you own a stock and you think it will go down, but you would like to sell it at a higher price even so. In this circumstance you can "buy a put." A put is the right to force someone to buy your stock at a higher-than-market price. You pay someone approximately $2 per share to stand by for up to nine months, ready to buy your stock at $30 per share even if it goes down to $24. What kind of investor sells a put? One who believes that the stock is going up and that he will never be forced to buy. The buyer of a put gets downside protection and pays for it. This is a dangerous way to make money. I suggest you use broker's instructions instead (see page 75).

Gold, although it does not result in income, can be subject to option sales. David J. Nelson, Vice President of Investments for Prudential-Bache Securities, talks of "waking up your gold investment" by selling covered options. The system is exactly the same as the sale of stock options. Once again, the option adds income to an otherwise non-income-producing asset; but the purchase of options is always a speculation.

Commodities

For high risk and (perhaps) high gain, commodities take

the prize. I do not recommend commodities for those in the wealth-building years because the two major essentials for success are constant monitoring and the ability to take a loss. Losses can be great and immediate. In fact, commodity traders are not called investors, but rather speculators.

There are three forms of commodity speculation: individual commodities futures (the most popular), pooled management syndicates, and options. Commodities futures permit you to buy a contract at a given price in the belief that on the contract date, the date you must pay and accept delivery, the price will have risen. If so, you will sell the contract at a profit. If not, you must either accept delivery or sell the contract at a loss. The purchase is usually highly leveraged, with only 5 to 10 percent of the purchase price actually paid in cash.

Market conditions affect commodities more than any other investments—you are truly "playing the market." Moreover, when the commodity is grain or livestock, weather and health conditions are additional factors. Commodity syndicates work much the same way as mutual funds do, and commodity options work like stock options.

Gold

Of course, for a hedge against inflation, gold is the ticket. When prices of goods and services rise, the value of gold rises with them. In highly inflationary times there is nothing better than solid metal. Silver is the little sister to gold and should be judged accordingly.

Gold is first and foremost a commodity. It is volatile and may be purchased and sold at will. Timing is everything and the buying and selling of gold options works in the same way as the buying and selling of stock options. The one who writes the option (sells), if doing so while owning the gold, has written a covered option and is really augmenting the value of his portfolio rather than speculating. On the other hand, if your plan is to speculate you will buy rather than sell gold options. You will pay money for the privilege of buying at a lower rate than you believe will eventually emerge. If gold does rise, you will exercise your option and sell at the higher price. If not, you will lose your option money. Nevertheless, for your speculation you can dabble with only a few hundred dollars.

There are many forms for the purchase of gold. You can purchase gold bars, bullion, and gold sheets from the bank.

Over and over again high marks are awarded to the purchase of gold coins. However, as with everything else there is a down side. A most important factor is expertise. Gold coins are valued both for their metal content and for their rarity. There are gold coins that are not rare and are bought only for their gold content. We'll take a look at these a bit later. For now, remember that rare coins should be purchased only by the connoisseur or through a company with a good track record, and with a certificate of authenticity awarded to the coin by the American Numismatic Association. Such certified coins are traded at auction and are virtually liquid. One can invest in them for as little as $500. The down side is that the market is volatile and one should expect to hold these coins for at least a five-year period. Naturally, all you would get is appreciation—no income, no cash flow.

The purchase of gold coins that are not rare can be made through banks and dealers. Popular coins are the South African Kruggerand, the Mexican peso, the Australian crown, and the old English sovereign, as well as the $20 United States gold piece and the Canadian Maple Leaf. These coins are regularly traded at a premium over the actual gold content. These premiums are small, however, because the coins themselves are not rare. You can follow the value of these coins by reading *Barron's*, which publishes the prices on a weekly basis.

Mutual Funds

The mutual fund is the average person's best way to play the market. A mutual fund is developed by a money manager who selects the portfolio of shares. Individuals or corporations can invest by buying shares in the fund itself rather than buying individual shares of corporate stock. This permits the small investor to make an investment in perhaps one hundred different companies at a time, giving him the kind of diversity he could not otherwise get. All that's needed to begin a mutual fund investment is $500 to $2,500.

Market management also comes with the purchase of mutual funds. The money manager is making the decisions, not you. You can liquidate your mutual funds at will, with one phone call. The amount you receive depends upon an independent evaluator who has been chosen by the fund; the evaluator sets fund prices at the end of each market day.

For the purposes of the consumer, funds are divided into two types, load and no-load. With load funds, a sales charge must be paid in order to become a member of the fund; no such sales charge is required for no-load funds. Because of this, load funds are supposedly anathema to the wise consumer. This is simply not the case. No-load funds often have hidden charges that make them more expensive than load funds. Find out what's behind the label. Does the so-called no-load fund take on a load when you leave? In other words, does the salesman get a percentage when you decide to sell rather than when you buy? Is the load staggered so that they receive less money the longer you leave your money in the fund? If so, you may be persuaded to stay with the fund in order not to incur a load. Are management fees raised by the cost of management, and is selling included in the management fee rather than in the sales commission? Only by knowing the answers to all of these questions will you be able to compare the costs to you of entering various funds.

Socially Responsible Investing

Expect to hear a lot about socially responsible investing in the next decade. Expect to hear a lot less about what it really means in terms of dollars and cents. Socially responsible investments fall into two categories: first, there are investments in companies devoted to cleaning up or preserving the environment, developing world peace, and insuring the survival of endangered species—in short, investments in companies concerned with the desperate issues of modern times; and second, there are investments in companies of any type that refuse to deal with nations, such as South Africa, that deny basic human rights.

As you can see, the former is a matter of "sector" investing, investments in special industries like the environment and global trade. The latter is a limitation on investing, excluding investments in companies that are not socially responsible. They are more a matter of conscience than investor strategy.

Mutual funds have become increasingly active in both areas. Many funds are now being marketed as environmental, global, or peace funds. The companies included are only those in a specialized field. Choose such funds based on past performance of the companies and of the mutual funds managers. Find them by contacting a broker and, as always, carefully read the prospectus that precedes all such funds sales.

Other funds will specifically state, in the prospectus, that they do not include companies that trade or do business with certain countries. The countries will be listed. Here it's important to note the politics behind the choices and the mechanisms for reevaluating political situations and national policies as times change.

Above all, the usual cautions apply:

- Read the prospectus.
- Judge by past performance.
- Know your goals.

Dollar-Cost Averaging

If you don't want to be concerned with moving in and out of a family of mutual funds, or timing your stock purchases, an investment strategy that yields good stock market results over time without monitoring is dollar-cost averaging. This is a systematic approach to investing that disregards current market conditions and emphasizes long-term growth.

A fixed dollar amount is invested on a regular basis. Investment shares are purchased and dividends are reinvested for growth. Fewer shares are purchased when the market demands a high price per share; more shares when the price is lowered by market fluctuations. Although shares of any type of investment may be purchased in this manner, mutual funds are often favored.

Over time, an investor may purchase more shares at a lower-than-market cost through dollar-cost averaging than if share purchases were timed to market conditions (see the table on page 86). In fact, the more volatile the market, the better your chance for reward.

Dollar-cost averaging is ideally suited for investors who have a secure, regular income and are disciplined to invest a fixed amount of money on a regular basis, monthly or quarterly. Let's take a look at an Individual Retirement Account (IRA) invested in a mutual fund portfolio. The investment is $150 per month or an annual investment of $1,800.

Dollar-cost averaging cannot prevent loss in a steadily declining market, but it can prove to be a very successful investment strategy, making the most of market fluctuations over the long term. It requires nothing more than the discipline to invest on a regular basis and a little patience. Long term, the dollar value of a dollar-cost averaged investment has a good chance to be worth more than the total amount of invested dollars. Investors can further reduce risk through investment diversification. Choosing a portfolio with a mix of common stock, bonds, and preferred stocks offers a greater protection against market risk than a common stock portfolio.

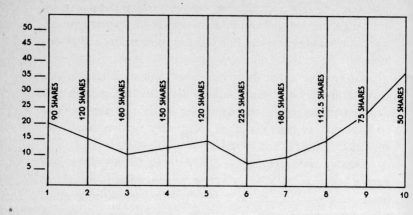

Year	Fixed Amount invested	Cumulative Investment Dollars	Cost Per Share	# of Shares Purchased
1	$1,800	$ 1,800	$20	90
2	1,800	3,600	15	120
3	1,800	5,400	10	180
4	1,800	7,200	12	150
5	1,800	9,000	15	120
6	1,800	10,800	8	225
7	1,800	12,600	10	180
8	1,800	14,400	16	112.5
9	1,800	16,200	24	75
10	1,800	18,000	36	50
				1,302.5 Shares

Based on the current market cost per share of $36, the original investment of $18,000 is now worth $46,890.

Unit Trusts

As investors have become more enamored of long-range planning, the unit trust has become a practical consideration. Like a mutual fund, a unit trust comes under expert management; little individual investor attention is necessary. Probably the most important feature of the unit trust is that the investor doesn't need to watch the market. Like mutual funds, the unit trust does fluctuate with the market. When the market goes down the net value of redeeming a share can go down. However, an independent evaluator (who should be separate from the trustee) makes a daily evaluation of the units.

The possible volatility of the unit trust should have little relevance to the investor in the right frame of mind—one who wants to place his money in a relatively conservative income-producing vehicle for a long period of time. The key to unit trust investing is that it is done for long-term gain, therefore any long-term fixed-income security (like a long-term bond) that can't be bought in small amounts is appropriate for a unit trust. The investor gets diversity plus the opportunity to invest in twenty or thirty bond issues. There is a ready market if the investor wishes to sell the shares. Shares are sold back to the trust itself, which redeems them and can then resell those shares. Usually a secondary market is made so that trades take place between the seller and someone else who has expressed a desire to buy.

There is one clear difference between unit trusts and mutual funds: a unit trust is close-ended, with no new shares being sold or created. Existing shares can be bought back by the trust and resold, but no new shares are offered. This is not so with a mutual fund. Mutual funds are managed and the securities are often sold and new ones purchased. With a unit trust, a trustee watches the portfolio and makes certain that the securities maintain sufficient quality. However, by and large there is no need for constant management since most of the securities are long-term and stable.

I had the opportunity to interview John Daly, head of the Unit Trust Division of Salomon Brothers, on the place of the unit trust in a wealth builder's portfolio. Although, says Daly, the unit trust investor is generally older than the wealth builder, with $25,000 or more to invest, a unit can be purchased for as little as $1,000. The small investor is much more likely to get a better reception from an account executive for a small purchase of units than he or she would when trying to buy a small number of bonds.

As the wealth builder begins to plan earlier and earlier in life, the unit trust becomes an interesting vehicle to save for children's education or for other easily identifiable obligations. Daly compares a track record of fixed-income mutual funds with unit trusts by looking at market history. Unit trusts grew dramatically in popularity in the late 1970s and early 1980s, when interest rates were rising and bond prices falling. In 1982 the bond market leveled off at a relatively high level, and 1982 to 1984 was a record time for the sale of mutual funds. Daly notes that in times of lowering rates, when the market is good, mutual funds do better because they can be more quickly moved to higher-paying fixed-income securities and do not have to remain with lower rates. A unit trust, on the other hand, does better when rates are rising and prices are lower, because the higher rates are fixed for a long period of time. Once again the key is in investor mentality. Are you looking for planning and security over a period of time (up to thirty years of locked-in rates)? If so, consider the unit trust.

THE ASSET GRADING SYSTEM

As you review your present assets or assess possible new investments, it is useful to have a handy grading system to see if the properties of the investments fit well into your personal lexicon of investment goals. In fact, the quality of your investments (the fit between goals to be achieved and money invested to achieve those goals) can be more important than the quantity of investments. Compare the "house-poor" suburban couple who can't take a vacation because their available cash is tied up in a down payment on their home with the retirees living in a trailer and seeing the world. Their net worths may be identical, but their life-styles are completely different, and each couple may be doing the most appropriate thing with their investment dollars in accordance with their personal goals.

To judge any investment you should have a score card. The best investment analyzer I've ever seen is Ronald W. Ady's *The Investment Evaluator—How to Size Up Your Investments at a Glance* (Prentice Hall, 1984). However, even this fine guide can be confusing for the eighteen to thirty-eight-year-old just starting out. The following analysis charts have been prepared with wealth builders in mind and make certain assumptions generally applicable to that group, with regard to which "properties" of investments are important; how the wealth builder will set his or her priorities; the wealth builder's level of expertise; and the wealth builder's ultimate goals.

The factors are:

1. liquidity
2. cost
3. leverage
4. income
5. monitoring expertise
6. tax
7. loss potential
8. appreciation profit

9. risk; volatility
10. usable as collateral
11. inflation fighter

The numbers on the right in these charts show how the characteristics of each factor rate for the wealth builder's special needs, on a scale of 0 to 10.

SAVINGS ACCOUNTS

1	total	+10
2	any amount	+10
3	none	0
4	low	+2
5	hassle free	+10
6	fully taxable	0
7	insured	+10
8	none	0
9	none	+10
10	all	+10
11	none	0

CDs

1	fair	+5
2	low	+8
3	none	0
4	good	+7
5	rollover consideration	+8
6	fully taxable	0
7	insured	+10
8	none	0
9	none	+10
10	90%	+9
11	none	0

MONEY MARKET

1	complete	+10
2	low	+9 (some minimums are required)
3	none	+10 (which makes for complacency)
4	fair for short-term investment	+8
5	none—which makes for complacency	0
6	taxable	0
7	low	+9 (amount of interest varies and some brokerage houses are underinsured)
8	none	0
9	low	+9 (interest varies)
10	good	+10
11	not bad	+7 (interest varies)

MUNICIPAL BONDS

1	great	+10
2	moderate	+6
3	good	+9
4	good	+7
5	low	+10
6	tax-free	+10

MUNICIPAL BONDS (cont.)

7	low	+8
8	numerical	+2
9	low	+10
10	good	+9
11	none	0

T BILLS, BONDS, AND NOTES

1	great	+10
2	high, bills	0
		(Bonds +5)
3	good	+8
4	good	+10
5	very little	+9
6	fed tax, no municipal	+8
7	loss potential	+10
8	very rare	+1
9	none	+10
10	good	+10
11	investment is short term so money will soon be available if interest rate increases	0

CORPORATE BONDS

1	total	+10
2	2000 share	+2
3	margin	+5
4	good	+8

CORPORATE BONDS (cont.)

5	moderate	+5
6	taxable	0
7	small	+8
8	none	0
9	low	+8
10	very good	+9
11	none	0

COMMON STOCK

1	total	+10
2	low	+8
3	margin	+5
4	dividend	+2
5	loss	0
6	taxable profit	+6
7	great but can use stop loss order	+5
8	great	+5
9	high	+2
10	SMA*	+5
11	none	0

*Supplementary Margin Account—an account the brokerage house is required by law to set up so that if your shares rise in value, your ability to purchase more shares of any type on margin increases. You're increasing your leverage because you can buy without laying out your own cash.

PREFERRED STOCKS

1	total can be restricted	+9
2	low	+8
3	none	0
4	good	+7
5	high, lots	0
6	capital gain	+6
7	great	+6
8	great	+5
9	high	1
10	SMA	+5
11	none	0

COMMODITIES

1	immediately salable	+10
2	no minimum	+8
3	margin	+8
4	none	0
5	a must	0
6	taxable profit	+6
7	the worst	0
8	the best	+10
9	the most	0
10	not much	+2
11	that's the point	+10

GOLD
(a commodity, but compare with above)

1	immediately salable	+10
2	no minimum	+8
3	margin	+8

GOLD (cont.)

4	none	0
5	high	0
6	taxable profit	+6
7	high	+4
8	high	+8
9	high	+3
10	moderate	+5
11	perfect	+10

COINS
(compare with above)

1	immediately salable	+10
2	no minimum	+8
3	margin	0
4	none	0
5	high	+8 (use a numismatic firm)
6	taxable profit	+6
7	more conservative	+6
8	great	+10
9	low	+9
10	moderate	+5
11	almost perfect (value is in condition and type of coin)	+9

Mutual Funds: rate as common stock, or whatever the underlying security, but give high marks to diversification and management.

Unit Trusts: rate as long-term bonds but give high marks to diversification and management.

SOME FINAL TIPS

With an understanding of the characteristics of various invest-ments, you can then make your plans without hesitation. Go back to the Goals Section (page 26) and remind yourself of what you are investing for in the first place. Is it growth or is it income? Is liquidity a key factor for you? Once you understand your needs you'll be able to see how investments compare with each other. Let's say, for example, that you are offered the purchase of a 7 percent municipal bond or a 14 percent second mortgage, in which you lend money to someone else and they pay you interest.

How then do you choose?

First determine after tax yield. If you are in the 15% or 28% bracket, the 7% bond will yield 7%. By contrast, the 14% mortgage will yield either 17.9% or 10.24% respectively. Next go more deeply into the other characteristics of the investments. The municipal bond may have a three-year maturity date; the second mortgage may keep your money illiquid for five years. The second morgage may not be as salable as the municipal bond. In such a case you are best off with the municipal bond.

Once you know how all these characteristics interact with your goals, look next at safety. Are you content with the collateral that's being suggested to you? Is the bond rating high enough? Is the house that's being purchased with your money sufficient collateral for you to lend? (Remember also that we are comparing two similar investments here: income-producing investments in which you are essentially lending money, in one case to a municipality and in another case to an individual.)

Perhaps it is growth investments that are being suggested to you. Once again, determine whether it is worth taking the risk associated with the growth investment. Apply the Rule of 72 that we have discussed earlier. Will your money double in substantially less time than if you simply invested for income under the prevailing interest rates? After you have determined that the risk/reward ratio is good enough for you, see whether the monitoring, volatility, and expertise needed are overwhelming to you, or if you feel comfortable with them.

Market conditions become important as you get more sophisticated in your investing. For example, in inflationary times we are concerned that our spending money won't go far enough. Perhaps then you will seek out an investment such as gold, whose major good point is that it is a hedge against inflation. If you don't see inflation ahead, you may want to keep your money in less inflation-sensitive vehicles than metals. After a while you will see that your needs and your goals change—at that point you should make a new net worth statement and re-analyze your holdings. Are they still right for you? It is no shame to sell and switch holdings. It would be as if you were expected to dress the same no matter what the styles were, or if you considered yourself reckless or stupid for not knowing five years ago what the fashion trend would be today. Keep up with the types of investments on the market and always look at their basic characteristics.

4

Understanding Your Job's Financial Rewards

You know by now that salary isn't everything when judging how much actual financial compensation you derive from employment. But what else is there? When investigating a job from the financial point of view, there are three important questions to ask:

1. What nonwage (nonsalary) benefits do I get?
2. What such benefits are available in general?
3. Can I get more of them elsewhere?

It is question number 2 I propose to answer for you by listing and explaining a variety of benefits offered by employers. A given company may provide some, but never all of these benefits. How will you know? Ask. Read the employee handbook of benefits before you accept the position, not after. Make a discussion of such benefits part of every interview when the topic of compensation arises. Show that you know the possibilities. Above all, do not accept a vague answer.

In my first book, *Moneythink*, I told a true story from my childhood, which bears repeating here. There has long been a popular T.V. game show called *Let's Make a Deal*. The game was to offer a contestant either a certain amount of money or the secret contents of a box. The excitement was fantastic. Should one take the money or the box? The audience would scream: "Take the box, take the money, take the box, take both!" After the choice was announced, the suspense really made your heart pound. If the money was selected, everyone hoped that there would be a bunch of carrots or a leek in the box. If the box was accepted, and turned out to be tiny, everyone hoped that inside there might be an automobile key. In every case the excitement was heightened by the element of risk. I was so fascinated by this game that I decided to play it with my mother.

I went to a local women's store and bought some handkerchiefs and gloves and put them in a box, and then I took a five-dollar bill and asked my mother which she wanted. But my mother hated the game. She didn't want me to spend five dollars, nor did she want to find out what was in the box. She spoiled the game because she did the one thing that was unexpected. She refused to play.

For a week the box lay, sealed with Scotch tape, alone and silent but conspicuous on our kitchen counter. Every day I would beg, "Please play the game. Do you want the box or the five dollars?" Every day she would say, "I don't like such games. If you spent a lot of money on things for me, I will be very angry." I had a terrible dilemma. If she thought I had spent money on her, she wouldn't play the game. If she wouldn't play the game, the box would never be opened. Every day I eyed that box and, even though I knew what was in it, I was eager to see the contents again. How could she be so incurious? How could she require such certainty? Finally I gave up.

I said to her, "There is less in the box than five dollars' worth of items." She looked at me and repeated, "There's less than five dollars' worth of items in the box?" I said, "Yes." "In that case," she said, "I'll take the five dollars."

Her refusal to make a choice until she knew the facts was

probably the best lesson I have ever learned. Don't make financial choices until you know all the facts, even if knowing the facts spoils the game that others are trying to play. To help you spoil the game, take a look at the following, which explains the types of benefits in store for you in a corporation.

IMMEDIATE OR SHORT-TERM BENEFITS

Bonus

This is a once-a-year reward for good performance. However, bonuses are not awarded by merit alone. Frequently there are formal rules and formulas for calculation. Many companies have a "norm award," that which is given to an average employee in an average year. Your actual bonus can range from 0 to 50 percent above norm, with a cap limiting your increase to 45 percent of your salary. Find out what the rules are and ask:

- If the bonus is limited to a percentage of salary.
- If the bonus depends on salary grade or classification (see below).
- If the bonus is measured by your individual performance, or by the overall performance of your division or section. Ask also if different bonuses have *actually* been awarded, or if lip service only is given to the merit criteria.
- If the bonus depends on your job title.
- If the bonus depends on the earnings of the company.

Some companies categorize employees by salary grade. Within a certain range of salaries each employee is assigned the same grade, although each earns a different amount. Usually this is much fairer when bonus time rolls around, especially for the wealth builder who will be eligible for a merit bonus even though he or she earns $5,000 to $10,000 less than a coworker.

Many companies have a limited pool of bonus money,

usually tied into a formula approved by shareholder vote. Ask for a copy of the plan. Most often, the fund is comprised of a percentage of profits above a certain level. This level is usually defined in terms of the value of the company. Ask if:

- The company carries over excess bonus funds to a lean year if they have an especially good year.
- The bonus fund is based on profits before or after taxes.
- If there is no carry forward in a good year, is the company committed to spending all the bonus funds in the good year? Frequently, the percentage of bonus funds used can vary. In such a company percentages are usually adjusted so that bonuses actually remain rather steady and predictable each year. Often the employee will begin to consider the yearly bonus as part of the salary. In other companies the amount is a surprise each year. However, some companies have an upside cap on the amount of bonus they give. Find out.

You may encounter the "golden handcuffs" approach, in which the bonus is deferred until you have been with the company a given number of years. (Boo!) However, do not confuse this with a deferral program, where *you* can elect to defer your bonus to another year. Ask:

- Can I defer the payment of taxes to the year of actual receipt of the bonus?
- If I leave or am fired, will I lose the deferred bonus?
- Do I get interest? (Generally you do.) How much?
- If my deferred bonus is invested, will the plan be good; how will it perform? Judge your company's investment portfolio as you would your own.

Even if these answers are satisfactory, remember, if the company goes bankrupt you're only a general creditor. Graef S. Crystal in *Questions and Answers on Executive Compensation:*

How to Get What You Are Worth (Prentice Hall, 1984) gives the following stunning example:

> Even though there are no golden handcuffs provisions in your deferral agreement, you could still lose your entire principal (and any interest that had accrued) if your company goes belly up. In such a case, you would become a general creditor of the company and would have to stand in line with the other creditors to receive your money. In all probability, you might only receive a few cents on the dollar. In the case of most companies, however, the risk of bankruptcy is, happily, quite low.

Stock Bonus

Some companies offer a stock bonus, for which all the considerations set forth above apply. Stock bonuses are especially important when considering long-term benefits; see page 104 for more on this.

A NEW LOOK AT SALARY

Salary must be considered by the wealth builder as a cornerstone of job acceptability. Salary structure can be more important than actual dollars in the first few years. Salary grades (the minimum and maximum salaries one can earn) are often the backbone of the structure. Grades, in turn, are based on either a *slotting* or *point factor system*. Ask which system is in use. Slotting is done basically by getting surveys and other information regarding salaries paid by competitors for each type of position. If you have some inside intelligence regarding the salary norms among industries, or within an industry, it can't hurt. If the point factor system is used by the company you're interviewing with, ask:

- What are the factors considered (for example, education, performance, attendance, age, number of subordinates)?
- How many points are assigned to each factor?
- Is the amount of money assigned to each point competitive with other companies you are considering?
- Are your strong points given heavy weight in the point system?

In determining how much salary increase an employee should get, companies usually consider several of the following:

- Your performance—placing you above or below the mid-point salary level for your position.
- Your present position, at the bottom or top of a salary grade. It's harder to get a big raise at the top of your grade unless you can step up to the bottom of the next grade.
- The company's "norm" salary figure.
- Future earnings forecast.
- Whether they give cost-of-living salary increases.

LONG-TERM BENEFITS

Of less immediate importance to the wealth builder, but of enormous future importance, is the offer of longer-term incentives. The one benefit that can affect all the others in this category is your becoming vested.

Vesting

You are vested in the company on the date at which you are absolutely entitled to money in the profit-sharing plan. Read each company's plan carefully, because they differ. For example, some plans allow for full vesting (entitlement to all the funds set aside for you in the plan) after five years of employment, so that 20 percent of the funds is vested in each of the first five years. Another plan may permit partial vesting after two years or three years.

The new tax law effects your rights to vesting. For the years after December 31, 1988 your company must provide for full vesting upon completion of five years of service or 20% vesting after two or three years and an additional 20% for each year thereafter. Ten year vesting will no longer be acceptable for a qualified pension plan.

Savings Plan

Some companies will match the money you are willing to place in savings. This matching contribution is also tax free, if placed immediately into the savings plan. Your money will be invested by the company; the types of investments differ and can include investing in the company itself as well as in outside funds. Here, too, your investment is managed and it is wise to compare the performance of the investment manager with, say, the performance of a large, well-advertised mutual fund.

Stock Bonuses

Stock bonuses can be a glory or a dangerous thing. You receive company stock instead of the usual cash bonus. Often the stock is transferred to you without cost as additional compensation, with no commission fees charged, or is offered to you at a favorble purchase rate. In either case there is ordinary income and you will have to pay immediate income tax, even though the stock does not yield cash to you immediately.

Ask the following questions: Are dividends reinvested if I defer receipt of the stock? In what? Are they used to buy more stock, or are they left as cash earning deferred interest? (I prefer the latter, but it depends on how strong you believe the company to be.) Deferring a stock bonus should result in your being taxed in later years, when you actually receive the stock.

The value of the stock on the date of receipt must be included in your gross income that year. It also becomes your basis in figuring capital gains if you sell.

Stock Options

A stock option is far different from a stock bonus. An option merely means a choice or a right to buy; regardless of what the present price is, the buying price will be fixed when the option is granted. The option permits you to buy the stock at a fixed price within a certain period of time. Options themselves are valuable and, as with real estate, they are often sold or traded. Many people buy and sell their stock options through brokers, making money not on the stock itself but on the buying and selling of the option. If you leave a company that grants options before your option period has expired and you haven't picked up your option, it is usually forfeited.

Sometimes there are restrictions on the stock that you purchase. For example, it cannot be sold to an outsider; or it must be sold back to the company; or upon the death of the stockholder the company must redeem it. Always compare the restrictions that the companies place on the stock as well as the value of the stock at the time that you are checking into the value of the stock option. These stocks certainly involve an element of risk. They are not the guaranteed money that the pension plan is. If you exercise your option and the value of the stock goes down, you are in the same boat as any other buyer of stocks. If you haven't exercised your option and the value goes down, you still haven't received any kind of benefit. You can negotiate a sliding-scale price, so that if the value falls, the stock option price is also reduced.

A stock option program that allows you to purchase shares

for cash won't be meaningful unless you have enough discretionary wealth. Use the Pay Yourself First Budget (Chapter 7) to make a stock option program a reality. However, do not take the easy way out and concentrate all your investing efforts in such a program, because it is generally illiquid and has the tax consequences described above. Measure each stock option purchase against the usual investment/goal criteria outlined in Chapter 3.

To determine how good a stock option program is in the early years of employment, ask:

- What happens when I leave?
- How soon can I exercise my option? (Usually it must be exercised within three months, although in some cases not for ten years.)
- Can I use appreciated stock options to buy more options so I don't always have to use cash?
- Does the grant of options depend on my performance, the performance of the company, or neither?

There are two types of stock option, the nonqualified type and the incentive type. Their characteristics stack up this way:

Nonqualified Stock Option	Incentive Stock Option
1. Taxed when exercised.	1. Not taxed when exercised (unless you are in the alternative minimum tax, see page 225).
2. Can be exercised in any order.	2. Must be exercised in order granted.
3. Longer option exercise period.	3. 3 months to exercise if employment is terminated.

Nonqualified Stock Option	*Incentive Stock Option*
4. Period of holding for long-term capital gains treatment is one year from date of sale of stock.	4. Period of long-term capital gain is one year.
5. Unlimited shares ca be granted.	5. $100,000 per year limit per employee.

Expense Accounts

Benefits such as cars, bonus trips, and even free financial counseling are sometimes available to the wealth builder, although they are perks more usually associated with those in higher executive positions. The benefit that often does apply to the wealth builder is the expense account. Is the company cheap or does it have deep pockets? When I interviewed for positions after law school, one Wall Street firm gave a coffee break and served cookies. Word got around to the senior class at my alma mater (New York University School of Law). Believe it or not, it was a popular concept, and resulted in almost our entire law review staff at least submitting resumes to the firm in question. Now, the brand-new wealth builder, coming from home where money is not plentiful, may be confused, perhaps deranged (cookies?!), when it comes to making choices. Please don't be lulled by the big expense account, breakfast meetings, or trips. By all means go for them *if* all other types of benefits are equal. Remember also the tax rules about expense accounts have changed drastically under the new tax law. Only 80 percent of meal or entertainment expenses are deductible. If you are reimbursed for the cost of a meal or entertainment, the percentage limitation will apply to the employer making the reimbursement. No deduction is allowed for expenses related to attending a convention or seminar unless such expenses are deductible as ordinary and necessary business expenses. In addition, deductions for travel expenses incurred due to travel as a form of education are no longer allowed.

Certain miscellaneous employee business and investment expenses will be deductible only to the extent they exceed two percent of your adjusted gross income. Included in this expense category are such items as investment advisory account fees, tax counsel fees, union or professional organization dues, tax preparation fees, and subscriptions to professional publications.

The new law also limits the deduction for expenses incurred in using the home for business to net income received from the business. Under old law, you could use the deductions against unrelated income, such as rent from your tenant. The new law also provides that a taxpayer cannot circumvent the limitations on home-office expenses by having taxpayer's employer lease a portion of the home.

- If the company pays directly to the hotel or whatever is owned—no tax to you.
- If you get a cash allowance—report it as ordinary income and pay taxes unless you can document actual out-of-pocket expenses. If you do so, this amount and only this amount can be used to reduce taxes, and only 80% expenditures.
- If you pay *more* than is reimbursed the IRS will likely disallow a tax deduction, considering the excess expenditure unnecessary for basics (you don't need a better hotel, luxurious car, or finer restaurant).

While you are getting the answers to all these questions about benefits, do a bit of judicious research yourself:

1. Get ahold of the company's proxy statements and annual reports for the past five years. Also get ahold of the proxy statements of some of the company's principal competitors.

2. Read the footnotes to the annual report that pertain to compensation plans. They will tell you the aggregate size of bonuses awarded for the particular year, and the various stock option and performance unit plans.

3. Read the company's proxy statements carefully. There you will find information on how much the most senior officers received in the way of salaries and bonuses. Be sure to read all the footnotes, because you may find out more there than in the remuneration tables.

4. Check the proxy statements for evidence of stock option grants, the size of grants made, and the frequency of grants made.

5. Go back through several years to see if you can find the text of the current short-term and/or long-term incentive plans. If you find them, construct some "what-if" scenarios and see how sensitive payouts are likely to be for varying levels of assumed future performance.

6. Turn to the proxy statements of the other companies. Read them briefly and try to form some conclusions as to whether the company you are considering joining pays well or is chintzy.

7. Find the back issues of *Business Week* and *Forbes* that report on executive compensation payments made to the top officers of a variety of companies. Again, draw some conclusions as to the relative pay levels being offered by your prospective employer.

Ultimately, balancing your salary, short- and long-term benefits, and day-to-day perks will facilitate your wealth building the most.

5

Preserving Wealth

TALKING TO YOUR PARENTS about their estate means cross-ing the last frontier of intimacy between them and you. It is not difficult to pinpoint the reasons for reluctance to discuss your parents' money. Are you showing yourself to be greedy? Are you acting ghoulish, looking ahead to their eventual demise? Are you admitting that they will die and stripping away your denial mechanisms? Are you just plain embarrassed by the issue?

Whatever the feeling, even the closest family becomes stran-gers when it comes to vertical (between generations) money planning. Nevertheless, there are many reasons that you should try to learn all that your parents are willing to impart. First, your parents most likely do not know how to plan their estate. Estate planning is the technical term that lawyers and financial planners use for helping people who are near or past retirement age to live well on the money they have accumulated, and eventually distribute what is left over to their heirs. It can do a lot more for the planner than for the heirs. If your parents were brought up to learn little about finance, they may not even have a will, and may never realize the consequences of this lack.

They may believe that each will inherit everything from the other even without a will. And they may be unaware of the tax saving potential in estate planning.

Your purpose in finding out your parents' plans, if you can, must never be to change their ways regarding money or financial planning. Such an approach would likely be considered meddling and would close the door even further to an understanding of your parents' financial situation. What can happen, however, is that in discussing matters with them you can teach them certain things that you will learn from this book and from other investigations that might make them realize they should consider some planning as well. Usually the "hot button" is your parents' concern about what would happen if they became ill or had to go into a nursing home. By sharing some of the information in this chapter you can open their eyes to protective measures they can take.

Finally, of course, it is for your own future planning that opening the conversation to money matters becomes important. Have they already made provisions for you or for your children? Is any money that they have transferred held in trust for you, in a Uniform Gift to Minors Act bank account (see page 124), or is it coming to you when you reach a particular age? Do they understand the tax consequences of the gift they have made? If something should happen to your parents, do you know where their bank accounts and bills are, and other important information? Do you have any special rights to Social Security or other benefits that you may not know exist and therefore will eventually forgo?

The culture in which we live and its legal foundation honors inheritance. Indeed, if our government passed a law tomorrow outlawing inheritance we would probably have another American revolution. If anyone were to tell your parents that upon their death everything they had accumulated must go to the state, there would be shock, anger, and a call for change. Yet this is exactly what happens to most Americans because they do no tax planning or estate protection planning.

ARE YOU LEGALLY
ENTITLED TO AN INHERITANCE?

What are the inheritance rights of children? If your parents make no will, state law will apply. Most states give approximately one half of an estate to children if one parent is surviving. Often, a basic lump sum (for example, $25,000) is given to the parent before the division is made. If the estate is less than this lump sum, the child gets nothing. If there is no surviving parent, the children usually share the estate equally. If one parent and several children survive, in many states the parent gets a lump sum and only one third of the remainder; the children share the other two thirds equally. Often, if both a parent and child predecease the other parent, a grandchild will take a share together with his or her surviving grandparent.

Once your parents decide to make a will, they can dictate the inheritance rights of their children, regardless of what the state law says. Many people believe that they are required to leave money to their children. This is not true in most states. In other words, you can be disinherited with aplomb.

If a divorced parent remarries, in most states the second spouse will inherit a greater amount of money, or perhaps the entire estate, over and above a child of the first marriage. If a parent has children of a second marriage, however, it is likely that by statute all of the children from both marriages will inherit equally. Again, they can also be disinherited.

ARE YOUR PARENTS
ENTITLED TO INHERIT FROM YOU?

Parents, too, have inheritance rights. I know one young man who is a millionaire (a computer game innovator); his mother doesn't have much of her own. Another young man (a well-known film star) of my acquaintance can, in the vernacular, "buy and sell his mom and dad." Because most children don't have this kind of money, very little thought is given to the rights of parents to inherit from their children.

But often an adult child is giving aid to an elderly parent. If so, the adult child may want to protect the parent in the remote event that he or she dies first. If the child has no will the parent inherits in accordance with the laws of the state where the child resides at the time of his or her death. This may mean that the parent, because he or she is a remote relative compared to a spouse, may get nothing. If there is no spouse, it is likely that the parent will inherit everything.

A parent can also be disinherited in the same way as a child. The child simply makes a will, leaving money to others. No money need be left to a parent. However, the right to disinherit a parent is limited to adult children, since in most states people under the age of twenty-one cannot make a valid will. This becomes unfortunate in some situations. An abusing parent may actually inherit from a child he or she has abused. As a result, some states (notably Connecticut) have actually instituted divorce proceedings between parents and children. Either the parent or the child can initiate such proceedings. If they are successful, inheritance rights are cut off.

Divorced parents retain their statutory rights to inherit from their children. If a divorced parent remarries, and has children from the new union, he or she has the right to inherit from all of his or her children. This is true regardless of the number of marriages. By the same token, the children can also disinherit the parent.

WHAT CAN A WILL ACCOMPLISH?

A will can help you focus on your finances and it can be a catalyst to financial planning. While it is only one document, it can take the place of many. This diagram of will substitutes shows the will as the hub of your estate plan. The outer circle shows the many devices needed to accomplish the same effect.

Section I of the "spoke diagram" shows that to leave your assets to particular beneficiaries you must give them gifts or make trusts during your lifetime. This takes the place of charitable bequests, marital bequests, and the residuary bequests.

Section II shows that to pick those who are your best fiduciaries (executors or trustees), you can research and interview during your lifetime and enter into various contracts and agreements with them, instead of having a will that names them. For most people, a will is a simpler approach.

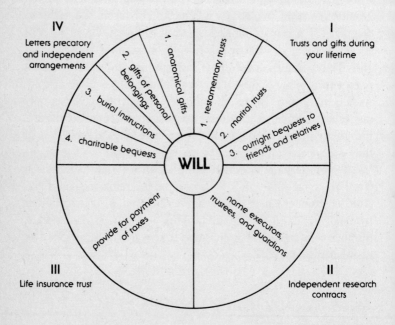

IV

Letters precatory and independent arrangements

2. gifts of personal belongings

1. anatomical gifts

3. burial instructions

4. charitable bequests

1. testamentary trusts

I

Trusts and gifts during your lifetime

2. marital trusts

3. outright bequests to friends and relatives

WILL

provide for payment of taxes

name executors, trustees, and guardians

III

Life insurance trust

II

Independent research contracts

Section III helps if you want to provide for the payment of estate taxes, which you will have with or without a will. You can do this through insurance trusts that pay the taxes for your estate, as long as the premiums are kept up.

Finally, section IV is useful if you wish to have special burial instructions or give your personal belongings to friends and relatives. You can do so by giving gifts or preparing a letter for your administrator. These are will substitutes. But there is no one document that can accomplish so much with respect to getting the right things to the right people as a will. It is true that probate (the legal determination of the validity of a will) can be expensive, but the substitutes for it are equally costly and difficult, if not more so. Furthermore, if you don't make a will, the government can end up choosing your beneficiaries for you.

HOW HAVE YOUR PARENTS TREATED YOU IN THEIR WILL?

There are standard will provisions that determine how you and your children will most likely inherit. Your parents will probably designate a *per capita* or *per stirpes* method of inheritance. *Per capita* means that the money is distributed equally among those individuals in the same relation to the parent (for example, equally among all the children). If one of them predeceases, his or her share is divided equally by the others. *Per stirpes* means that if one of the children dies before the parent, his or her heirs (grandchildren) divide up that share. Literally, the heirs sit in their deceased parents' "stirrups" and inherit by their right. Here are examples:

> Per capita: Three children are beneficiaries. If one dies, two divide his or her share. If the deceased child had children, they would get nothing.

Per stirpes: The same three children are beneficiaries. If one dies, his or her share is divided equally between his or her children. The two surviving children keep their original share.

Personal Property

Another item in the will that may affect you particularly is the personal property clause, covering tangible items such as jewelry, paintings, and the like. Specific stocks, bonds, and other cash substitutes may also be bequeathed under this clause. The moving expenses, if any, related to the gift are the responsibility of the legatee (the person receiving the bequest), unless the will specifies otherwise, as are liens against the property (documented rights that a creditor has in the property). Therefore, you will not inherit free and clear, unless your parent so provides. An example of a personal property legacy is: "I give my gold pin with three emeralds to my daughter Nancy if she survives me."

If your parents leave you a specific piece of property, they are not obligated to keep that property for the rest of their lives. Many people who bequeath their gold earrings, say, think that they must change their will if they lose one of them, or if they decide to cash them in because the price of gold has soared. Not so. If you die without owning that specific piece of property, the legatee will simply not get anything. This is called ademption or a "failed bequest."

To ensure that a bequest doesn't fail, you can state that in the event the personal property no longer exists the legatee will get the dollar equivalent, or another gift that you also describe.

Letters Precatory

Particularly if parents have more than one child, there can be good reasons for leaving out specific bequests. The alternative to announcing the facts in a will is the "letter precatory."

This is a handwritten letter signed by the parent and given to the executor of the estate. It can list all the odds and ends of personal property, both valuable and sentimental, and whom they should go to, without publishing this information in the will. The executor, of course, must be someone whom you can trust to carry out your wishes.

Alternatively, the will can permit the executor, particularly if he or she is a spouse, to divide things up at his or her discretion. For example: "I leave my doll collection to my beloved daughters, and direct my husband, John, as executor to divide them among our daughters at his absolute discretion, having due regard for our daughters' preferences. John's decision shall be binding and conclusive."

To make life easy, personal property can be left in a general way:

> I give, devise, and bequeath all my jewelry, clothing, books, personal effects, household furnishings and equipment, automobiles, and other tangible personal property, wherever situate, which I own at the time of my death, together with my insurance policies, to my children to share and share alike. In case of a dispute, the decision of the executor shall be final.

Are You Still a Minor?

Typically, a minor child's share of an estate will be left in trust with the surviving spouse as trustee. Minors themselves (under eighteen or twenty-one years of age, depending on the state in which they live) cannot act as fiduciaries. With a substantial trust, a professional trustee (a lawyer, bank, or trustee company) is preferable.

Children also typically receive bequests through a custodian when they reach a specified age. This contrasts with a trust because there is no distribution of income to the child's guardian during the period of minority. The bequest "vests" (belongs to the child) immediately, but the custodian controls the funds. If a child is to receive a share in a business or investment portfolio, the parent should designate a fudiciary, perhaps the executor, to manage the assets.

If, instead of an outright gift, a trust is created, the maker of the will must decide whether to create one single trust for all of his or her children, or separate trusts for each child. The consequences of this decision largely have to do with taxes and administration. Both solutions can provide for the sprinkling of income to the children at the trustee's discretion or, instead, for its accumulation. Principal can be invaded by the trustee for education purposes and for emergencies. The separate trusts can terminate and the funds from each can be distributed to each heir at different dates. A single trust will also terminate at a specific date and be distributed to each child at different specified times.

The single trust (often called a "pot" trust) is useful in a small estate, where bookkeeping for several trusts would be too expensive. Furthermore, if the income is small, the tax bracket will remain low despite the lumping of all the bequests into one trust. On the other hand, with a large estate, separate trusts divide the funds among many children and create several low-income taxpayers.

TRUSTS AND GIFTS

Wills are not the only way in which your parents may have provided for you. Trusts and gifts are another. You should know the difference between them and a little about your ownership. First of all, here are some useful definitions.

Trust Terminology

> **Trust.** A written document, the purpose of which is to put your money in the hands of a third party so that the third party can use it only for the benefit of your loved one.

Trustee. The person to whom you give the money, so that he or she can handle it for your loved one.

Beneficiary. The person to whom you wish to leave your money.

Corpus. This is Latin for "body," but here it means the money itself or the bonds, stocks, diamonds, or whatever else you wish to give to the trustee for the benefit of the beneficiary.

Settlor or grantor. The person who creates the trust (you).

Revocable trust. A trust that the settlor can revoke and stop.

Irrevocable trust. A trust that the settlor cannot terminate; it goes on without control by the settlor once it has been made.

Inter vivos trusts. The Latin literally means "between" (inter) and "living persons" (vivos). These are trusts that you create during your lifetime. You can even be the trustee. The trust can terminate on your death or during your own lifetime. One that you create during your lifetime can "pour over" into another trust in your will so that it continues even after your death.

Testamentary trusts. These trusts are created only by will and come into action only upon death. They are part of a last will and testament. If there already is an inter vivos trust, one can instruct in the will what to do with it.

How a Trust Builds Wealth

A trust, then, is a device that creates a new taxpayer, the trust itself. This taxpayer may be in a lower bracket than the settlor/grantor. If funds are accumulated in the trust, the tax rate and tax bracket that apply to the trust apply to the income derived from the investment of the funds. If income is distributed to the beneficiary, then the beneficiary's tax bracket and rate apply to the income derived from those funds. In either case, a trust will reduce taxes and increase wealth if the trust or the beneficiary is in a lower tax bracket or taxed at a lower rate than the grantor.

The following chart shows how trusts work in your will and during your lifetime.

INTER VIVOS	TESTAMENTARY OR TRUST IN WILLS
Saves on estate and income taxes. Allows you to see how your fiduciaries control and use funds.	Controls the use of money even after death. Allows long-range tax planning.
Takes effect during your lifetime.	Takes effect at your death.
Gives property away irrevocably if estate taxes are to be saved.	Property remains yours during your lifetime.
Can be revocable; but no estate taxes will be saved.	Property is taxed along with the rest of your estate.
Can save on income taxes because they will be paid either at the trust's rate or at the beneficiary's rate.	No income tax advantage.

THE NEW KIDDIE TAX RULES

The Kiddie Tax applies to children from birth through age 14. Under it, the first $500 of a child's independent income is not taxable, while the next $500 is taxed at the youngster's rate of 15%. Any additional unearned income is taxed at the parent's marginal tax rate. Parents can report their children's income on their own tax return if: the child has only interest and dividend income; the child's income is over $500 and under $5,000; and no estimated taxes or back-up withholding for the year was paid under the child's name and Social Security number. If these conditions are not met, then parents must file Form 8615 on behalf of the child. Children over age 14 pay at their own tax rate, as do children with earned income of their own.

Starting in 1988 the first $5000.00 of trust income is taxed at 15%, beyond that a 28% tax applies. Therefore, accumulating income in a trust instead of paying it out to the beneficiaries will save a maximum of $650.00 (28%–15% [13%] of $5000.00) if the beneficiary is in the 28% bracket. In fact, if the trust is a big one earning between $13,000 and $28,000 a year in income, there is a 5% surcharge, further reducing the income tax benefit of the trust. Result? A chilling effect on accumulating income in a trust fund.

Second, the Clifford trust is virtually eliminated. This was a major device through which young parents could invest for their child's college education. The plan was to transfer excess savings (perhaps from a pay yourself first budget) into a trust naming the child beneficiary of the income, but giving the parent all the principal back in 10 years or more. In this way, the income was taxed at the child's lower rate and could grow faster and accumulate for college.

Under the new law, the reacquisition by the parent (grantor) of the principal results in taxing the income at his or her income tax bracket all along. There is no shift to the lower bracket taxpayer.

Finally, if a child under 14 years receives unearned income, i.e., as a result of an investment made for him or her by a parent in excess of $500 per year, the so-called Kiddie Tax applies. The first $500 is tax-free because the child can apply the standard deduction to unearned income. The second $500 of unearned income is taxed at 15%. Unearned income of a minor child in excess of $1,000 is taxed at his parents' rates.

There is a presumption that assets come from parental sources unless the taxpayer demonstrates otherwise. Assets received by the minor either directly or indirectly from a parental source fall within these rules. However, property received on the death of a parent constitutes nonparental source property. Earned income is taxed at the child's rate.

Special Trust Provisions

In defining goals and creating trusts, it is not only the financial aspects of the trust provisions that parents think about—it is the administrative provisions as well. A lot of this depends upon the personality of the child, or at least what the parents perceive the personality to be. Some special provisions of interest to parents are the spendthrift provision, the accumulation provision, and the Crummey provision.

"Spendthrift trusts" are a creation of the rich, who found that their spoiled children often spent trust income before it was distributed to them. Creditors such as jewelers and automobile dealers were often willing to accept a marker giving them the right to collect future trust-guaranteed income. Would-be heirs often had all future income pledged to creditors. A spendthrift trust protects these people from themselves; it doesn't give them any interest on the income until it is distributed, so they can't give it away beforehand. Such trusts can also empower the trustee to make only direct payments for the needs of the beneficiary, instead of giving him or her income.

The Crummey provision grew out of one of the more famous cases in trusts and estates history. The result of the Crummey case is that if you do create a trust, your beneficiary can demand up to $10,000 a year from it, which is then considered the same as your giving a gift of that amount. Such a gift is completely tax free. It is not included as income to the gift getter, nor is it included in determining a gift tax or estate tax for the gift giver. In making a trust with a Crummey provision, you are actually creating another donor who is entitled to give $10,000 a year tax free. This newly created donor is the trust itself.

To take advantage of the Crummey, a beneficiary need only demand the $10,000. However, there are simple limits to this provision:

1. The beneficiary can demand the $10,000 only once in any calendar year. If he or she permits the year to go by without demanding the money, that year is up and the money can no longer be paid.

2. The beneficiary will get the money only if a transfer is made by the grantor to the trust itself.

3. Each year the trustee must give the beneficiary notice of the right to withdraw and a reasonable opportunity to exercise the right.

In case your beneficiary does not call for the $10,000 gift and lets it lapse, the Internal Revenue Service considers this a gift by your beneficiary to the trust.

The Remainder Interest

There is a final and quite sophisticated method of transferring funds to your children for the purpose of saving estate taxes. Technically this is called a sale of a remainder interest. It works this way. Mom and Dad own a home worth $300,000. They wish to live in that home all of their lives. Yet they do not wish that $300,000 to be counted in their final estate. If they give the home to their child and continue to live there and use the property, there will be a gift tax to pay. If they leave the home to their child in their will, there is an estate tax to pay. If, on the other hand, they sell the remainder interest (the right to full and complete ownership after death of the parents) to their child, there is quite a tax saving.

First of all, a reasonable price should be set for the sale. The price need not be as high as the fair market price, since there is a substantial discount when the parents retain life occupancy. The child's right to own does not take place until after the parents' death. When the sale is made, no gift taxes are paid. When the parent dies the child acquires the property through sale, not inheritance, and no inheritance tax is paid.

Where does the child get the money to buy the remainder interest? The sale can be made on an installment basis, or the child can even set up an annuity for the parent. Of course, the parent would leave the money received from the child to the child in the will and this could be taxed. Nevertheless, when the smoke clears the parent has saved half of the estate taxes that would have resulted without use of this strategy. The child has paid the parents and the value of the home at the time of their death is not included in the estate for estate-tax purposes.

Note: If the parent had died owning the home and left it to the child, no estate tax would be saved but the child would receive a "stepped-up basis" (when the child sold his profit would be based on the differential between sale price and value at the time of the parents death). An installment sale prevents such stepped up basis but saves estate taxes. As you can see, these are highly technical alternatives and a lawyer must be consulted to work out all the details.

The Uniform Gifts to Minors Act

There are special ways of giving gifts to youngsters, for example, the ever popular Uniform Gifts to Minors Acts, which has been enacted by every state and is uniform nationwide. Perhaps you have been the recipient of a gift under this act. Any adult can make a gift of securities in bearer or registered form, or a gift of cash, to someone who is under the age of twenty-one when the gift is made. To make the gift, the parent merely delivers the funds to a custodian for the underaged donee. The custodian can be any adult member of the minor's family, a guardian, a trust company, or a lawyer. If the gift is of securities in registered form, money, life insurance policies, or annuity contracts, the donor can also be the custodian. If the gift is an unregistered security, the donor cannot be the custodian. The custodian has very broad powers to hold, manage, or invest this property. His or her duties include the usual fiduciary responsibilities, such as registering the securities or placing the money in a specific account, and keeping good records for inspection. The custodian can sell or exchange the property and use the proceeds for the minor.

The donee receives the money upon reaching the age of

twenty-one. If he or she should die before age twenty-one, the money would become part of his or her gross estate. Once given, the gift is irrevocable; it belongs to the donee. Although the custodian (or donor) is empowered to control and manage the money, any tax due from earned income is taxed according to the rate for the trust, and not according to the custodian's personal income. If the donor dies before the minor reaches age twenty-one, however, the property will accrue to the donor's estate and estate tax will have to be paid.

The following chart shows the tax-saving advantage of the Uniform Gift to Minors Act.

Pro	Con
• Some income from the investment is taxed at the lower income tax rate of the donee.	• The gift is irrevocable— once given it cannot be taken back.
• The use of the money (and the income from it) can be controlled by the donor throughout the minority of the donee; this includes using it for the health and welfare of the donee.	• If the donee should die an early death the money will be taxed in his or her estate.
• The gift will automatically go to the donee at age 21 so that the right person is going to receive the funds.	• If the donor should die before the minor reaches 21, the money will be taxed in the donor's estate.

Joint Gifts

Two kinds of gifts can be set up jointly: joint tenancy and tenants-in-common. A joint tenancy creates ownership of the entire sum in both parties. Both you and the donee own the whole gift. Neither can sell or otherwise transfer his or her half without the participation of the other. Neither may use the property as collateral without the other's knowledge and consent. If a parent creates a joint tenancy with a child and the child dies, the amount will be fully inherited by the surviving parent; if the parent dies first, the amount is fully inherited by the child.

By contrast, tenants-in-common each own a half interest in the property. If one dies, his or her heirs inherit, not the surviving half-owner.

Parents often create joint ownership between themselves and a child or grandchild. In fact, many of us do this without realizing we are creating joint gifts. Here are a few examples:

1. A joint bank account opened in your name and a child's (or other's) name. A gift is considered to have been made (and tax incurred) when the other party withdraws money. No tax is incurred if each party contributed an equal amount.
2. Purchasing a United States Bond in two names. The purchaser may cash in the bond tax free; the other party would pay a gift tax upon cashing in the bond.
3. Purchasing joint stock. Naming a joint owner establishes that a gift has been made.
4. Putting real estate in another person's name. A gift is considered to have been made when the new deed is issued.

If a parent and child are joint owners and one of them dies, the amount of holdings added to the decedent's estate is determined by who purchased and contributed to the holdings. (It may thus be possible for all the holdings to be considered part of the estate of the first to die.)

Custodial Bank Accounts

Many people open up an account in their own name together with a minor. For the most part, this is the creation of a joint account. There is confusion as to the proper method of taxing such an account. At least one tax court has held that interest earned in joint tenancies is taxable to the owners in proportion to their contribution. Another court held that the contributions were immaterial and the taxes were to be placed on an equal basis. For the most part, the former will be the case since the government will view these joint accounts as remaining in the control of the adult. A court order is needed to make changes, withdrawals, and other decisions.

One point to caution you about: frequently, a lower-tax-paying grandmother will, without informing her children or grandchildren, set up a joint account. The interest from that account is money that she expects to declare and pay taxes on at her lower tax bracket and rate. If the Social Security number of the child is listed first, however, the government may consider the funds to be that of the child, and precipitate an audit on the unsuspecting child.

USE INSURANCE AS A FUTURE NEST EGG

Recognizing that there is no one best investment, most financial planners acknowledge the need to diversify. But the question always arises, diversify in what? Mutual funds, real estate, treasuries, CDs, zero coupon bonds, etc.? I'd like to propose a different alternative, which if used properly can become one of the best investments you'll ever come across. However, to understand and apprecate it fully you may first have to overcome some self-imposed emotional barriers.

The idea I'm proposing is to own a life insurance contract on one of your parents, and then have the proceeds, which come due tax-free, either be owned and used by yourself or be placed in a trust owned by your children. These proceeds can then be invested in either a fixed-income or variable-interest investment, or a combination of both. In this way, you can easily generate in excess of a million dollars in your lifetime, or put your children in a much stronger financial position as they start their families.

There are only three instances in which an individual can own a life insurance contract on another person: you can take one out on yourself or another family member; business partners can take them out on each other; and so can anyone who has an insurable interest in/on another person. (This does not include, for example, friends, employees, ex-spouses, or lovers.) There are no other opportunities to legally own or be a beneficiary on anyone else's life.

For years, parents who were business owners have recognized this opportunity and have been using life insurance proceeds to help pass on a tax-free lump sum to their sons or daughters upon their death. This has not been the case with parents and children who do *not* own a business, although it quite certainly can and should be used. Let's assume you're age thirty and have a parent who's age fifty-five. The cost to purchase and maintain a $100,000 life insurance contract until the parent dies at or before age eighty is an average of $1,500 a year, or $125 a month. What this means is that should your parent die at any time during the next twenty-five years you will receive a lump sum of $100,000 income tax free. This would mean that by age fifty-five or earlier you'd have an additional $100,000 available for investments. It should also be noted that while I have funded for and assumed that an individual will live to age eighty, this is statistically not usually the case.

There are many assumptions that can be made; however, they are beyond the scope of this book. The point to keep in mind is that this program provides an opportunity to create $100,000 tax free (or fractions or multiples thereof), in addition to any IRA or other investment program you may already have. This program provides the maximum amount of flexibility to either stop paying the monthly premiums and have the contract pay for itself through internal accumulated funds, or to simply discontinue the program and recover the following dollar amounts:

Years paid in	Amount	Available at surrender
10	$15,000	$12,000
20	$28,000	$24,000

To learn more about how this program can work in your specific situation contact Henry Montag at 200 Park Avenue South, Suite 1408, New York, N.Y. 10003. Include your name, address and telephone number, together with your parents' ages and whether or not they smoke. Henry has prepared a free detailed analysis of how this program can be put to work using the approach that would be the most cost-effective in your specific situation. While the numbers are based on good health and a nonsmoking parent, the absence of these factors should certainly not deter you from further exploration.

The point to keep in mind is that most parents and grand-parents would certainly be interested in assisting their children by either splitting costs or matching their children's share to help create a trust fund for their children or grandchildren—if only they were given the opportunity to do so. It's up to you to present them with the idea, however. I urge you to further explore this opportunity as it makes a great deal of sense.

6

Secrets
of Money
Management #1:
Buy Real Estate and Don't Sell It

WHEN THE VARIOUS PROPERTIES OF INVESTMENTS are analyzed, real estate emerges as perhaps the most perfect and desirable. Why? Since real estate, properly chosen, generally increases in value, there is potential for growth and appreciation and little potential for loss. Rent-producing real estate, whether commercial or residential, meets the criterion of high income guaranteed by the underlying lease and secured by the right to evict if necessary. Real estate is probably the most easily leveraged investment, for mortgage money is available if you know where to look. Further, real estate once purchased is a great source of collateral—for a second mortgage, equity loans, refinancing first mortgages. While income derived from real estate is fully taxable, it affords certain tax savings which can balance the inclusion in income. Finally, the value of the real estate inevitably rises in inflationary times, largely because real estate is the one investment that is also a necessity. So why doesn't everyone run to buy real estate? If you listen to casual cocktail party talk, you'd presume that they do! Everyone seems to own a co-op, condo, house, residential or commercial property, or all of the above. Why not you?

Perhaps the answer to this is that without knowing the rules of investment analysis you instinctively understood the difficulties of real estate purchase, especially for the younger investor. They are:

- cost—even a 20 percent down payment can be out of reach; a mortgage may be too high a burden on cash flow; or tax savings and income don't equal the outlay.
- liquidity—if you must sell, it will take more than a phone call to do so.
- monitoring—managing real estate can be a full-time job and you don't have time.

This chapter will teach you how to buy real estate and make money at it despite the above drawbacks. But you will still be left out of the most perfect investment ever if you suffer from *real estate phobia*. Perhaps my greatest contribution to you will be to expose this little-understood and deadly disease, and help find a cure.

OVERCOMING REAL ESTATE PHOBIA

Life Regret No. 1: It is a snowy winter day in 1974. The real estate market is at an all-time low. I am taking my weekly excursion to the Connecticut countryside to find a country house. There it is—five acres, a long entry drive, the back of the land leading down to a natural stream rushing with cold water. The house is small, but it has a fireplace of stone, a brand new kitchen, two bedrooms, and it's in good condition. I look around. Looks fine to me. The price: $47,000. And then I see these five dead ants on the floor. Ugh, I say. The house has ants. I offer the very low figure of $38,000. The broker sheepishly calls the seller and says, "I have a very low offer of $38,000." The seller says, "Are you kidding? Nope, we're staying at the $47,000 figure." I say, "Okay, not interested." I leave. Fade out.

It is 1980. I am taking my usual excursion to the Connecticut countryside to look for a country house. I find it—same house, same two bedrooms, same ants. The price: $175,000. Just sold.

Or does this sound familiar to you:

It is 1974 and you are looking for a place in the city. You are sick and tired of spending $450 a month rent for a one-bedroom apartment with a view. You find a two-bedroom co-op. It is very small. The asking price: $18,000, nonnegotiable. The maintenance fee is high—at $450 a month, you're not saving anything from that rent money. And what is a co-op anyway? You vaguely know it's not real estate but you're not quite sure what it is. Well, you think you'd better let it go and just keep renting. After all, you won't have to make your own repairs. Fade out.

It is 1980: same apartment, same two bedrooms. Maintenance has risen considerably—it is now $600 a month. The resale value: $175,000.

The rest is history.

Why weren't these properties purchased? Because of real estate phobia, which I am convinced is a psychological as well as a financial problem. It is harmful and burdensome and the disease is suffered by many and varied people. Everybody talks about real estate, but few discuss the innate fear that most people have of burdening themselves with it. This is especially true for the first-timer who has never purchased before.

I first became aware of the depth of real estate phobia many years ago at what was then called a "consciousness-raising group." The concept of marriage itself was in turmoil, and somehow everything that was worrisome about marriage was symbolized by the "purchase of the house." Many women in the group said that they had no fear of getting married, but they couldn't bring themselves to buy a house. Two people said that when they did go to buy a house, the week prior to the closing they had thoughts about death and finality.

From a financial and a psychological point of view, many

people look at the purchase of real estate as a final step. They see it as something that is physically big (rarely, if ever, will you be able to buy an item larger than a house), that is very expensive (rarely, if ever, will you buy a single item that costs as much as a house, particularly one that is mortgaged with interest payments accumulating over thirty years), and that cannot be readily resold. Unlike jewelry, a painting, or a fur, a house takes a good percentage of your income each month. You cannot merely buy it, be extravagant, and forget about it. Rarely do you pay cash for a house, and therefore the responsibility goes on.

Part of the cause of real estate phobia is ignorance. The cure must begin with overcoming resistance to buying your own home. A young couple who are clients of mine have made and broken several appointments. Both of them work; both of them have substantial income. They have no children. They suffer badly from real estate phobia. Every day they study the real estate ads. Every weekend they take a trip to look at a different parcel of real estate. During the week they wonder whether they should buy or not, and at the end of the week they are again on the road, looking for something new. They cannot make the final decision.

To overcome this problem, the following steps must be taken.

1. Understand that there are many right choices. Real estate phobia stems in part from the incorrect belief that there is only one right answer. People are so terribly confused about the differences between co-ops, condominiums, and houses that they cannot decide among them. They may also believe that it is financially shrewder to live either in the city or in the country, in a duplex or in a ranch house. They have the idea that if only they could choose the precisely correct piece of property, they would make a million dollars. Under such decision-making pressure many people make no decision at all, and let each parcel of property go by the boards. The answer is

that there is no one right decision. There are wiser decisions and poorer decisions, but there is no single decision that is best.

2. Set priorities. You must establish your priorities and know what you are willing to give up. A good friend of mine and one of the most successful real estate speculators in the country pointed out to me in my early days of understanding real estate that if I had a million dollars to spend I would have the same problem that I have with ten thousand or a hundred thousand; that is, I would have to give up something. Frequently I leaf through a magazine called *International Homes*, in which few of the homes pictured are under a quarter of a million and most are over a million. It's a wonderful education—I can actually look at a million-dollar house and say, "Gee, I don't like the way that swimming pool is shaped or where it's placed." *There is no perfect home*; you will not find it for a million dollars and you will not find it for fifty thousand dollars.

3. Decide what to spend the right way. Ultimately it is the money—the amount of it and the financing—that solidifies the real estate phobia. "How much should I spend? How much should it cost?" become the operative questions. But there are no *shoulds*. In choosing a home, you must look at your personal budget to determine what you can "spend." One misconception must be buried for all time—the idea that people show their wealth through the size and appearance of their home. In choosing property for investment, you look at the income that you will obtain and the money you will earn.

Not long ago the rule of thumb was one should spend 25 percent of one's income yearly on shelter. This has changed drastically because of inflation, and has moved up to 33 percent. Again, this is a *should*, and the only should is that we should eliminate shoulds. What do you want to spend every month on shelter? You already have made that decision once, since you are living somewhere right now. When you can make that decision again independently on any other question, without having found a house and without looking, you have answered your preliminary question about what price range you are in.

4. Do not sell your first house; rent it to someone else when you want to move. Most Americans are used to planning for ever-increasingly burdensome home ownership. The scenario usually goes as follows: Young couple borrows from family and adds their own savings and buys small house. Their income, needs, and assets grow. They find a new, larger, more expensive home and scramble to sell their first home. Finally, after much trauma, they get a buyer. All the appreciation and all their accumulated capital is put into the new, larger home. They are house-poor again. This happens twice more until they retire, sell their last home and wonder why they did it all in the first place!

However, if you can manage not to sell your first house, but to rent it when you move, you'll then enjoy the following scenario: Young couple buys first home as above. Income grows, as does home value. They take an equity loan using the increased equity in their first home as collateral. They find a new house and use the equity loan as down payment. Their second house has been chosen in accordance with how much they can earn by renting their first house. They move to the second house and use their rental income, usual mortgage money, and some additional income to pay both the mortgage on the second house and the equity loan on first house. They watch *both* these properties appreciate in value. They do this twice more. Finally they retire, sell all the property, and wave good-bye as they sail off on their world cruise!

Let's take a closer look at how to buy your first home and your investment property.

HOW TO BUY REAL ESTATE

Choosing It

There are two types of real estate purchases that any investor contemplates—a purchase for his or her own residential or business use, and a purchase for investment purposes. The considerations for the two types are very different. In both cases location is the key to good selection. However, a good location for a house in which you will live with your children is considerably different from a good location for making a profit. In my book *Your Kids, Your Money* (Prentice Hall, 1984), I suggest evaluating the following location-related factors in buying your own home if you have a young family.

Quality of schools in the area
Number of children in the classroom
Student/teacher ratio
Quality of textbooks
Availability of computer equipment in the school
Status and background of the principal
Comparative reading score of the school (the local board of
    education should have this information)
Age of the schools
Safety in the area
Number of crossing guards
Proximity to parks, libraries, and religious institutions
Proximity to museums and other cultural centers
Traffic patterns, including those caused by industrial parks
    in the area
Time taken from your children because of your commute to
    work

A single person would be more interested in the following considerations.

Proximity to work
Safety
Neighborhood vitality
Restaurants in the area
Other entertainment

In evaluating location, you must look for a neighborhood where the prices of the other parcels in the area are higher than yours. This gives you the opportunity to build your own nest, put in a hot tub, a new kitchen, etc., and not lose money on the renovation. If you are investment-minded rather than "dream"-minded, you can give the place a coat of paint and resell at a higher competitive price. You must also purchase in a neighborhood that is ascending in value in general, not descending. Most people are frightened by this requirement. How can they know if a neighborhood is increasing or decreasing in value? Ignorance in this area may be the greatest cause of real estate phobia. Relax—most neighborhoods increase in value. With the continued shortage of housing, it is more likely that you are going to find a rising neighborhood than one that is lowering. Certainly, part of the decision is instinct. But it is highly unlikely that you will go wrong. Look at the zoning, public areas, schools, support services, and transportation. Trust yourself. Ask the broker for a neighborhood report—they will tell you what houses have sold for recently and compared to the last three years. This information is not a secret.

Second to location, condition is the most important consideration. Don't be discouraged by an outrageous paint job, the need to move a few shrubs, or even having to put in a new kitchen. *Do* be discouraged by poor sewage, bad plumbing, a defective structural beam, excessively repaired leaks. Get an inspection and make sure it is more than a cursory one. Have your realtor make a recommendation for an engineer, and also call a few from the Yellow Pages. For specific information write to American Society of Home Inspectors, Suite 520, 1629 K Street N.W., Washington, D.C. 20006.

Finally, practicality—in other words, price—enters the picture. Part of the value of real estate benefits is the tax deduction derived from interest payment deductions. Therefore, your tax bracket is an important factor in determining how much you can actually pay. For a small fee ($5.00), the Department of Consumer Economics and Housing will determine if you are better off renting or buying given your tax bracket, income, and other data (write them at MVR Hall, Cornell University, Ithaca, New York 14853). In the long run, though, almost everyone is better off buying their own home *unless* they have plans to put their money into real estate for investment, and cannot afford to do both.

There are many rules of thumb for home buying, but they change over the years. A survey shows that the average middle-class, middle-income couple spends 35 percent of their gross yearly income on their total housing costs. The old rule was 22 percent. Mortgage markets use a rule of thumb in which the cost of the house should be no more than 2½ times your gross yearly income. Most mortgages cover 80 percent of the purchase price and vary considerably. Another way to look at this is that it should cost you one and a half weeks' salary for every month of carrying expenses—mortgage, taxes, PITI (*P*rinciple *I*nterest *R*eal Estate *T*axes *I*nsurance).

Because of inflated costs you may not get the home of your dreams. In *The Power of Money Dynamics*, noted financial planner Venita VanCaspel offers the following maximum home purchase prices and relates them to gross annual family income.

Gross Annual Family Income	Maximum Home Purchase Price
$15,000	$36,000 to $43,250
$20,000	$45,000 to $54,000
$25,000	$54,500 to $65,000
$30,000	$64,000 to $76,000
$35,000	$72,750 to $86,750

Gross Annual Family Income	Maximum Home Purchase Price
$40,000	$81,750 to $97,500
$45,000	$91,000 to $108,500
$50,000	$100,000 to $120,000

Notice that she expects the $100,000 to $120,000 home to be purchased by a couple earning at least $50,000. This home may not be much more than the $50,000 home of ten years ago. Should you become "house poor" to achieve the American Dream? Perhaps buying a smaller home in a safe area and sending your children to private school is a better alternative for you. Don't forget to count hidden expenses such as a gardener, a new roof, rising utility costs, and regular maintenance. Home buying involves more costs than just a mortgage and down payment.

Buying a home also proves the old rule that nature abhors a vacuum. Furniture tends to jump from stores into your living room. This is clearly part of the fun; it is also part of the cost. On the other hand, real estate taxes and interest on the mortgage are tax deductible.

Once you have found a home with the right location, condition, and price, *buy it* and *don't sell it!*

If you are concerned with choosing purely investment property you must add a fourth criterion to judging your purchase—yield. There are four basic formulas you can use to calculate real estate investment yield depending on your orientation. If income is your priority, try this:

$$yield = net\ income \div purchase\ price$$
(net income = annual rental income minus all annual costs)

If return on capital (your down payment) is of interest, try this:

$$yield = net\ income \div cash\ down\ payment$$
(net income = annual rental income minus
annual costs minus annual mortgage)

If return on capital plus the building of equity is important, don't reduce the rental income by the amount you have paid off on the mortgage *principal* per year, since that principal becomes part of your growing equity in the property:

yield = net income ÷ cash down payment
(net income = annual rental income minus
annual cost minus mortgage interest)

If tax savings are important, try:

yield = net income + tax savings ÷ cash down payment
(net income = annual rental income minus
annual costs minus mortgage interest)
(tax savings = tax bracket × net taxable income)

Here are the four formulas computed for the following example.

Purchase price = $120,000
Down payment = $20,000
Net income = $17,200 (annual rental income)
            minus $5,000 (annual costs)
Mortgage principal and interest = $10,200
Mortgage interest = $8,000
Net taxable income = $1,800
Tax bracket = 50%*

(**1**) yield = $17,200 − $5,000 ÷ $120,00 = 10.17%
(**2**) yield = $17,200 − $5,000 − $10,200 ÷ $20,000 = 10%
(**3**) yield = $17,200 − $5,000 − $8,000 ÷ $20,000 = 21%
(**4**) yield = $17,200 − $5,000 − $8,000 + 50% × $1,800 ÷
       $20,000 = 25.5%

*Naturally, your tax bracket may be 15%, 28%, 33%, plus any state taxes which bring you above the top federal level.

Negotiating Price

This is perhaps the hardest part of buying for the new investor. Getting the feel for negotiation and being ready to walk away from the project if your offer isn't accepted is rough stuff for most of us. At the beginning it is comforting to know that real estate fortunes are not made because of low purchase prices, but because of high sales prices and rental income in between. If you overpay a bit, the market will eventually make it up to you. It is also comforting to know that even major real estate tycoons often use a broker to transmit messages regarding purchase price.

Because the real estate agent is compensated only if the buyer and the seller close a deal (unless, after contract, the seller refuses to "close title," or transfer ownership), the broker tries to make the parties agree on price. Legally the broker is agent for the seller because his commission is paid by the seller. However, an intelligent broker takes care of the buyer's needs or no deal is made. In many communities, houses are multiple-listed. This means that every agent has the same homes to sell. The initiating agent and the agent who actually makes the sale share the commission, which runs to about 6 percent of the selling price. Occasionally a short exclusive right to sell is given to an agent.

Your real estate lawyer may negotiate for you; our office does this regularly. But be honest with your lawyer. State whether you *must* have the property or can walk away from it. A fair rule of thumb (which can certainly be broken over and over again) is to offer 25 percent below the asking price and settle for 15 percent. This is hard bargaining. Special situations where the rule of thumb would not apply include:

a dilapidated house
a divorce situation
an estate
the first house to sell in a development
the last house to sell in a development

Once the price is set, the next steps are contract and closing.

Contract and Closing

Here is where the attorney for the buyer and the attorney for the seller come into the picture. Their jobs are simple—they have nothing to do with the purchase price, and they will not advise you whether you got a good deal or not; they just work out the contract of sale. This contract is a form document printed by the local real estate board, with blanks throughout that need to be filled in. One of the most important items is correctly entering the names of the parties. This contract is a prelude to the deed, and if a name is not on the contract it may be left off the deed as well.

After the names of the parties, the contract states the description of the property. Next comes the purchase price and the fact that you have given a deposit, usually 10 percent. It goes on to state whether or not you are seeking a mortgage and, if so, the terms of the mortgage; for example, a 70 percent mortgage for a thirty-year period at an interest rate of 13 percent. Included will be a statement that if you do not find this mortgage, you will not have to buy the property. This is very important. It permits you to get out of the deal without penalty if you should be turned down for a mortgage. This is why so many sellers are interested in selling property to buyers who have the cash to pay.

The contract will also state what personal property in the house will remain. This usually includes appliances, kitchen cabinetry, and bathroom fixtures, sometimes the curtains and sometimes shades, and sometimes much more depending on the deal you have made with your seller. The agreement will also provide that your right to the property is subject to a title search by a valid title company (to be explained shortly). If after a title search you find that the seller does not have good title, you can get out of the whole deal, again without penalty.

Your contract will also provide that you are taking the property subject to certain restrictions. For example, you are responsible for knowing the zoning laws. If you want to buy the property to open a business and you discover after the deal goes through that it's only zoned for residential use, you are stuck with the property. You are also required to take the property subject to anything that a survey will show. A survey may show that there is an easement through your property belonging to somebody else. This means that someone else has the right to walk through your property. The agreement might also provide that you shall inspect the property and that if you are not satisfied with the inspection you will get out of the deal. An inspection is usually done by a professional engineer or real estate inspector. You, the buyer, are responsible for paying for the inspection. Don't expect to find everything that is going to go wrong with the property for the rest of the years you are there. It often happens that the month after purchase an undiscovered leak comes to light. But you will get a general idea of the heating system, the plumbing system, and the foundation of the home. You will probably also have a termite inspection, which you will pay for separately. If the building is in treacherous condition or there are termites, you might not want to buy the property, or might want to bargain for a lower price. This can be done even after the contract is signed.

FINANCING

For people in the wealth-building years this is probably the toughest part of real estate ownership—getting a down payment and getting a mortgage.

What Is a Mortgage?

A mortgage is the security that the lender (mortgagee) holds on the real estate owned by you, the purchaser (mortgagor).

Lenders consider a mortgage on a personal residence the most stable loan that can be made. (This is based on the assumption that an individual's financial situation would have to be desperate before he or she would fail to maintain the payments on the home.) If you elect to buy a home, the debt for the money is represented by the note you and your spouse signed at the time the mortgage loan was made. When there is a failure to pay the debt, the mortgagee sues. A judgment on the note is then enforced by commencing foreclosure proceedings against the property. In most states foreclosure on a first mortgage takes about a year. During that time the mortgagor may pay the debt and terminate the proceedings. In some states, even after foreclosure the mortgagor has the right of redemption. This means that for a specified period (usually six months) after foreclosure the mortgagor may pay the mortgage and reclaim the property.

Lenders are not in the business of owning property. They are in the business of lending money. If illness or loss of a job prevents you from meeting your monthly mortgage payments, they will not foreclose but will work out a payment plan.

Mortgage selection has become complex because of the numerous types of mortgages and variations in rate schedules. To learn about the various types of mortgages, write for a free copy of "The Mortgage Money Guide," Federal Trade Commission, Sixth and Pennsylvania Avenue N.W., Washington, D.C. 20580. For now here is a quick glossary of mortgage types taken from the manual.

- **Fixed-Rate Mortgage** Fixed interest rate, usually long term; equal monthly payments of principal and interest until debt is paid in full. Offers stability and long-term tax advantages; limited availability. Interest rates may be higher than other types of financing. New fixed rates are rarely assumable.

- **Adjustable Rate Mortgage** Interest rate changes are based on a financial index, resulting in possible changes in your monthly payments, loan term, and/or principal. Some plans have rate or payment caps. Readily available. Starting interest rate is slightly below market, but payments can increase sharply and frequently if index increases.

Payment caps prevent wide fluctuations in payments but may cause negative amortization. Rate caps, while rare, limit amount total debt can expand.

- **Renegotiable Rate Mortgage (Rollover)** Interest rate and monthly payments are constant for several years; changes possible thereafter. Long-term mortgage. Less frequent changes in interest rate offers some stability.
- **Balloon Mortgage** Monthly payments based on fixed interest rate; usually short term; payments may cover interest only with principal due in full at term end. Offers low monthly payments but possibly no equity until loan is fully paid. When due, loan must be paid off or refinanced. Refinancing poses high risk if rates climb.
- **Graduated Payment Mortgage** Lower monthly payments rise gradually (usually over 5–10 years), then level off for duration of term. With flexible interest rate, additional payment changes possible if index changes. Easier to qualify for. Buyer's income must be able to keep pace with scheduled payment increases. With a flexible rate, payment increases beyond the graduated payments can result in additional negative amortization.
- **Assumable Mortgage** Buyer takes over seller's original, below-market rate mortgage. Lowers monthly payments. May be prohibited if "due on sale" clause is in original mortgage. Not permitted on most new fixed-rate mortgages.
- **Seller Take-back** Seller provides all or part of financing with a first or second mortgage. May offer a below market interest rate; may have a balloon payment requiring full payment in a few years or refinancing at market rates, which could sharply increase debt.
- **Buy-down** Developer (or third party) provides an interest subsidy which lowers monthly payments during the first few years of the loan. Can have fixed or flexible interest rate. Offers a break from higher payments during early years. Enables buyer with lower income to qualify. With flexible rate mortgage, payments may jump substantially at end of subsidy. Developer may increase selling price.

The following worksheets provided by Weichert Realtors will help you plan your financing by giving you answers to the questions most frequently asked by people between the ages of twenty-one and thirty-five.

How Much Money Will a Bank Lend Me?

INCOME - QUALIFICATION

Borrower	$ _____	
Co. - Borrower	$ _____	
Other or Employer subsidy	$ _____	
Total	$ _____	
÷ 12 = monthly gross	$ _____	
Mo. Gross × 28%	$ _____	(A)
vs.		
Mo. Gross × 36%	_____	
(−) Debts	_____	
=	$ _____	(B)
Lower of A or B	$ _____	

This is the amount most lenders feel should be an affordable and comfortable monthly amount to cover PITI.

Is purchaser **comfortable** with this amount?

Has the Tax Shelter Impact of Acquisition been considered?

Monthly payment from above	× 12 Months
Total Annual Mortgage Payment	_____
Minus (−) Annual Insurance	_____
Minus (−) Annual Principal	_____
Interest & Taxes (Deductible)	_____
Estimated Tax Bracket (see page 148)	× _____ %
Estimated Tax Savings (Annual)	_____
Divided (÷) Monthly	÷ 12
Estimated Tax Savings Monthly	_____
Monthly Mortgage Payment Prin., Int., Tax, Ins.	_____
Minus (−) Estimated Tax Savings	_____
Net Housing Expense	_____

How Much Should I Borrow?

DETERMINING PRICE RANGE

Qualified PITI Amount (from above)		$	_____
(+) Employer monthly subsidy (if applicable & not already considered)	+	$	_____
Total to cover PITI		$	_____
(−) proposed tax (monthly)	−	$	_____
(−) proposed H.O. Ins. (monthly)	−	$	_____
Monthly Amount For P + I		$	_____
(÷) Mortgage Factor (Variable - see tables)	÷		_____
Mortgage amount	=	$	_____
(+) Down payment Available reduce by anticipated closing cost)	+	$	_____
Total Available for Acquisition		$	_____

TAX RATES* MARRIED
FILING JOINTLY UNDER THE NEW LAW

Two-Rated Structure: 15% and 28%

1987, rates (married filing jointly):

$	0 − $ 3,000	11%
	3,001 − 28,000	15%
	28,001 − 45,000	28%
	45,001 − 90,000	35%
	above $90,000	38%

1988 and future years, rates (married filing jointly):

$	0 − $29,750	15%
	above $29,750	28%

Indexing for inflation will begin after 1988.

The 15 percent bracket would be phased out for high income taxpayers. A 5 percent surcharge would apply to that portion of taxable income in excess of the minimum amount specified in each range:

$71,900 − 149,250 for married filed jointly.

---

*This table is intended to provide approximations for purposes of tax planning. Actual tax liability should be calculated by reference to IRS tax tables and rate schedules.

Alternative I

Monthly Amount for P + I	$	_____
(÷) Mortgage Factor (Variable - see tables)	÷	_____
Mortgage amount	= $	_____

Alternative II

Monthly Amount for P + I	$	_____
(÷) Mortgage Factor (Variable - see tables)	÷	_____
Mortgage amount	= $	_____

What Are My Monthly Carrying Charges?

Proposed Purchase Price of Property $ _____
(−) Cash Investment
(Downpayment)   − $ _____
Amount to be financed   = $ _____
Amount of 1st Mortgage or Assumption $_____
    Terms: _____
    Factor per M per month _____
Monthly Payment . . . . .A) $ _____
Includes: ☐ Princ ☐ Int
          ☐ Taxes   ☐ H.O. Ins.   ☐ MIP
Amount of 2nd Mtg or Add'l Dwnpymt Loan $ _____
    Terms: _____
    Factor per M per month _____
Monthly Payment . . . . B) $ _____
Includes: ☐ Princ ☐ Int
Plus (if not included above)
☐ Taxes (1/12th of Annual)   C) $ _____
☐ H.O. Ins (1/12th of premium)   D) $ _____
☐ Other. . . . . .E) $ _____
Total Monthly Investment
(A + B + C + D + E) . . . . $ _____

Should I Take a Fixed or Adjustable Rate Mortgage?

I don't know, but the following computer companies do:

- Shelternet. This system from First Boston Corp. (Park Avenue Plaza, New York, N.Y. 10055) lists more than 250 mortgages available throughout the country. It also determines how large a mortgage a homebuyer can afford and whether he or she qualifies for a specific mortgage. If the homebuyer qualifies, Shelternet conditionally approves that loan and seeks verification of information the buyer has provided from employer, bank, credit bureau, and house appraisal firm. Loan institutions pay the Shelternet fee.

- Realtors National Mortgage Access. Nicknamed Rennie Mae, this service is operated by the National Association of Realtors and is available from participating members. The system currently provides terms and conditions from lenders in the San Diego metropolitan area only. But any lender is welcome to provide information, and NAR expects the service to go nationwide by the end of 1986.

- Two other services describe different types of mortgages available in specific areas. HSH Associates (71 Madison Street, Pequannock, N.J. 07440) covers New York, New Jersey, southern Connecticut, central Florida, and southern California. Peeke & Associates (101 Chestnut Street, Gaithersburg, MD 20877) concentrates on Maryland, Washington, D.C., and environs, and southern Florida. Each firm issues weekly reports costing $10.

I do want to interject a word of caution about adjustable mortgages. They can be better for the wealth builder than fixed-rate mortgages. They may be assumable, which increases the salability of the house. Furthermore, interest rates may eventually go down and you might enjoy a reduction in your rate. But beware, for many beginners are lured into *very low* rates for the first five years with larger, escalating rates in later years. This is no way to try to afford a home, and will only give you ever-increasing burdens.

Taxes and Finance

The true cost of your financing can't be determined without a tax calculation. This extra factor is discussed in Chapter 11, where we look at how Uncle Sam relates to wealth builders.

Down Payment

Where does the wealth builder get the initial down payment for his or her first piece of property (usually 20 percent of the purchase price)? Here's a checklist of choices to consider:

_____I'll use my other investments as collateral to borrow down payment—they are:

_____

_____

_____I'll seek a personal loan from a bank to which I am connected, such as:

_____

_____

_____I'll ask for an intrafamily loan from:

_____

_____

_____I'll use the Pay Yourself First Budget (see Chapter 7) and target a savings of _____ per month by eliminating items _____ and _____ so I can have $_____ for a down payment by _____.

_____I'll go to my professional organization, union, or trade association to see if they make loans.

WEALTH BUILDING THROUGH REAL ESTATE

Much mystery surrounds the process of wealth building through real estate. However, with ordinary luck and much motivation, you can make real estate work for you. To do so you must take the following seemingly easy steps:

1. First, purchase a commercial or residential property that you do not intend to occupy.

2. Hold the property until at least 20 percent appreciation has occurred, or until at least 20 percent of the mortgage principal must be paid off.

3. This appreciation or reduction of mortgage will result in increased equity in the real estate. (Equity is the amount of before-tax profit an owner will have if the property is sold and the entire mortgage is paid off.)

4. A bank or other lender must extend a loan based on the increased equity.

5. The amount lent must be reinvested as a down payment or partial payment in other real estate.

6. This new purchase must result in income sufficient to pay the additional loan on the first purchase and pay the new mortgage on the second purchase; *or* the tax savings together with the rental income earned must be sufficient to pay that amount. The income-producing real estate may need a manager if you don't have time. Companies will act as a management for approximately 10 percent (or less) of the rent collected.

7. The procedure should be repeated often.

8. All tax consequences must be considered. The value of interest deductions depends largely on your tax bracket. The high wage-earner in the 28 percent bracket will save 28 cents for every dollar deducted; the wage earner in the 15 percent bracket will save fifteen cents for every dollar.

Co-ops and Condominiums

Don't be confused by co-ops and condominiums as alternative forms of shelter. They are viable forms of ownership. A condominium permits you to own an apartment in the same way you own a home. You buy it outright, take your own mortgage, and analyze your ability to pay in the same way as you do with a house. In addition, you will have partial ownership as a tenant-in-common of certain shared spaces and facilities—for example, the laundry room, hallways, garden, and pool. You pay a monthly maintenance to the building association to keep up your share. This should be equal to or less than the upkeep (gardening, snow removal, roof repairs, and so forth) of a single-family home.

A cooperative is a different form of ownership and is not considered real estate. But it provides the same shelter. Here, you own shares in a corporation. The corporation owns the building and sometimes the land. You take a co-op loan to pay for the shares. The corporation takes a mortgage to pay for the building. You as a shareholder pay maintenance to keep up the premises but also to pay off the corporation's mortgage. Usually about half of your monthly maintenance payment is tax deductible, because it represents your share of real estate taxes and interest payments on the mortgage. To determine affordability, compare the price of the share, the monthly maintenance, and the tax savings with other alternatives, for example, a single home or a condo.

Fee Simple Real Estate

This type of ownership gives you the unbridled right to sell the property, use it as collateral, give it away, or leave it to someone in your will. Fee simple real estate is usually purchased with a bargain and sale deed and owned alone or with another. When husbands and wives own real estate, they are automatically considered to have the special rights of joint ownership. This means that one of the owners cannot sell, give away, or bequeath the property or use it as collateral for a loan without the knowledge and consent of the other person. One half of it can't be left in a will to a former wife or a child or friend, so that you end up being partner with someone you dislike. Joint ownership can have the "right of survivorship." No matter what a will says, if one person dies the surviving joint owner has the automatic right to inherit the whole piece of property. Frequently deeds to real estate provide for joint ownership with right of survivorship.

Stocks, bonds, bank accounts, co-ops, condominiums, certificates of deposit, and almost anything that you can think of other than tangible personal property can be owned jointly with right of survivorship. This gives unwed people the best protection around. If you are a joint owner the law does not look at the other relationships between the parties. It couldn't care less if the parties were living together or hardly knew each other. The law upholds the rights of joint owners without question. They are entitled to everything from an accounting to each other, in case there is income being produced by the property, to full disclosure if one party is foolish enough to try "secretly" to use his or her share as collateral for a loan.

If you are buying the property with another person, you may not want to be so tied down with respect to ownership. Maybe you would like to be free to give away, sell, or leave your half to someone else. Or perhaps both of you would like to be more independent. You can have that too, but of course you get less security. You can own the property instead as tenants-in-common, which means that every bank account, share of stock, bond, real estate co-op, etc., will have both of your names on it, but instead of saying "joint tenants" it will say "tenants-in-common." Each of you does own half of the property, but you are free to sell your half, give it away, use it as collateral, or leave it in a will. There is no right of survivorship. Your mate can end up owning only half the property with some stranger. As I said, less security, more flexibility.

REIT
(Real Estate Investment Trusts)

These are mutual funds whereby the investor owns shares in companies that in turn own real estate or land mortgage money and receive interest. The advantages are:

1. High income (taxable)
2. The small amount of money it takes to buy in—usually $2,500, and $500 per share thereafter
3. A ready sales market—REITs are traded on the major exchanges like stock

4. Chance of good appreciation of your shares
5. Good hedge against inflation

In the mid 1970s REITs did very poorly because of a real estate market decline which I believe we will not see again. Our office encourages all wealth builders to invest in one or more of the following types of REITs:

Equity—this type buys income-producing property and is an investment with good appreciation
Mortgage—this lends money to others and is a high-income investment
Hybrid—combines all of the above

To learn more about methods of purchase and comparison, write to the Audit Investment Realty Stock Review, 230 Park Avenue, New York, New York 10017, or send a stamped 8½ – 11" self-addressed envelope to Henry Montag & Associates, 200 Park Avenue South, New York, New York 10003, requesting REIT information for the latest in the field.

Shared Housing

Of all the new trends, perhaps the most exciting is that of joint or shared housing, which is also referred to as Co-Housing. This is the movement which expands the concept of cooperative and condominium ownership to include shared healthcare, childcare, and recreational facilities. Even co-op food-buying ventures and credit unions can be part of these new-age housing developments.

There are many models. At the forefront is the Co-Housing experiment that began in Norway. Individually owned homes and cluster housing are concentrated around a pedestrian mall. Health- and childcare facilities are accessible to the community.

Inhabitants are of all ages. But this is more than a place to live; it's a way to live. Concepts of the extended family, of mutual reliance, and of intergenerational interaction take Co-Housing beyond real-estate ownership. To learn more, read *Co-Housing* by McCamant and Durrett, available by writing to them at 48 Shattuck Square, Berkeley, California 94704.

Newsletters and organizations that track trends in shared housing, including finances, legal aspects, and availability, are burgeoning. Ads for affinity groups are often found in the classified section of various newsletters such as *L.A. Co-Ops & Shared Housing Networker* (P.O. Box 27731, Los Angeles, California 90027), which also holds seminars and conferences.

Soon we will see advertisements by land developers and architects who will be building shared housing over the next decade. The high cost of housing, the need for mutual facilities, and the desire for urban and suburban families to be less isolated and autonomous are catalysts for a boom in this type of housing. The fierce independence of the average homeowner, the reluctance of banks to finance, and the very newness of the concept are the factors that may hold expansion back.

I predict this trend will catch on. Those developments that provide environmental beauty and preservation along with feelings of structural privacy will flourish best. Legal concepts like land trusts that permit individual ownership of the home and co-interest in the land are the most viable because they build on the familiar principles of condominium and co-op ownership.

Mortgage Investments Limited Partners

This type of investment is usually offered by financial services organizations when builders or developers need to borrow money to finance their projects. It allows an investor to reap the rewards often reserved for a major lending institution. The benefits are as follows:

- The opportunity to collect 2 to 3 percentage points of the money lent when a builder borrows money for a project.
- The opportunity to share in the appreciation of a property once it is sold or refinanced.
- The opportunity to share in the increased income revenue from a project during the term of the mortgage.
- The opportunity to be guaranteed both current as well as deferred interest of approximately 10 to 13 percent during the term of the mortgage.

This investment is suitable for IRAs, Keoghs, and pensions as well as for private investors. The usual life of the program is for five to ten years, depending on the project. This program can either be diversified in several different mortgages or can be concentrated in one individual mortgage, often at a higher guaranteed rate.

Public Storage Limited Partnerships

Public Storage is an opportunity to own a diversified portfolio of twenty to twenty-five mini-warehouse properties, which purchase land and build facilities to store commercial or residential goods in twelve to fifteen different states. Each program has a value of approximately $20,000,000. Each facility within the course of its seven- to ten-year life is expected to earn enough income to cover all expenses as well as generate a positive cash flow to the investor of approximately 10 to 15 percent per year after three to four years of its operation. The percentages then gradually increase to 15 to 25 percent in the fourth to seventh years.

In addition, it is anticipated that when the properties are ultimately sold in the eighth to ninth year there will be a significant increase in the value of each property. Approximately 75 percent of this increase is then proportionately distributed to the investor depending on the percentage of his or her ownership in the program.

This program is generally offered in two forms. The first buys properties for approximately 80 to 90 percent cash, thereby offering a greater degree of safety, a higher level of income, and virtually no tax write-offs. This combination is best suited for IRAs, Keoghs, and pension plans.

The second program purchases similar properties with less of a cash down payment and more leverage. Thereby it offers its investors a degree of tax sheltered income due to the interest write-offs as well as a current flow of income. Both programs offer the investor an opportunity to participate in the future appreciation of the underlying properties once they are ultimately sold. These programs are therefore commonly referred to as "land banks." They are ideally suited for the long-term investor looking for growth with no need for immediate liquidity.

Real Estate Public Limited Partnerships

This is a program whereby the general partners collect a large pool of investment dollars, generally in the vicinity of sixty to eighty million dollars from its individual or corporate limited partner investors. This money is then used to purchase leveraged residential and commercial properties in ten to fifteen states. The partners then either purchase or build a diversified portfolio of properties. They then collect rents for a period of time, generally eight to ten years, and ultimately look to sell their properties at a profit. Since leverage is used, this investment generates interest deductions as well as depreciation, which is then passed on as a tax-sheltered investment to its limited partners.

These investments should only be considered by individuals who can commit their dollars for long-term periods, usually ten to twelve years, as there is generally no opportunity to liquidate these investments before the holding period expires.

Timesharing

Timesharing is a fairly new concept of ownership. Several owners have the right to occupy the real estate, usually a vacation site, for a designated period of time each year. I own three timeshare weeks at Gurney's Inn in Montauk, New York. I tell you this to show you that I like timesharing, but *it should never be bought as a real estate investment.* There are no tax deductions, no income (unless you rent your week), and no guarantee of appreciation (you may eventually sell your week but there may not even be a market for it). So why did I buy three weeks? Because:

- Once you pay the price for a week (between $4,000 and $15,000), timeshare gives you free accommodations *every year*, in perpetuity—and prices at good hotels have risen as high as $200 per day.
- I wanted a place near the beach without buying a home, since I already have two.
- I'm cheap; once I pay for something I use it. These are forced vacations.
- I write books and I need a retreat now and then.

See, my reasons are not entirely economic. I do not want you to be fooled by promises of appreciation. Many down-on-the-heels resorts are trying to bail themselves out by "going timeshare." If you would like to buy, here's some advice:

1. Check the cost of staying in the resort. If the cost of the timeshare week is more than six times the cost of a week at the resort, don't buy.
2. Can you get to the resort without expensive air fare?
3. Do you have room for friends and family to go with you?
4. What are the hidden costs, i.e., cleaning charges and yearly maintenance fees.

5. Do you have financing?
6. Who has the ground maintenance contracts (pool, restaurant, etc.); what is their reputation? They will be with you long after the seller is gone.
7. Do you get an actual ownership? The prospectus should read much like a co-op prospectus and you should receive some form of ownership, usually shares in the corporation that owns the timeshares.
8. Is there a reciprocal arrangement with other timeshare resorts, so you can switch your vacation site and get variety?

There are basically three types of timeshare ownership. First there is the *fee ownership*, like a condominium. This is better than a cooperative and probably the best of the three. You will more likely be able to use the investment as collateral, and it is true legal ownership in real estate. A second form of timeshare ownership is a *right to use*. You can often buy this for the period of your lifetime, but it reverts back to the seller after your death and you have nothing to leave your family or to sell to someone else. The third and final form of ownership is a simple club membership, probably the least valuable. It does, however, get the developers away from having to file a prospectus with the state in which they are operating. Be warned that general club memberships are the cheapest but are probably never going to be an appreciating investment. You may not even get the same room or unit with such club memberships, just a swap for another.

Naturally, the possibility of reselling the timeshare at a profit shouldn't be taken for granted. To maximize the possibility of resale profits, purchase at the end of a project. You may save between $1,500 and $5,000 of the cost of a unit by doing so. The developer certainly does not want to keep on a major staff and its attendant costs to sell a few units.

The best idea is to buy for pleasure. Even so, you must

think about value. Buy from a project that has been in existence for several years. Make sure that the developer has prior experience in building, development, and ownership, and perhaps in resort management. Finally, make sure that there is management company in place under a reasonable contract, so that after everyone has purchased a unit you don't have to go shopping for some unknown management.

REAL ESTATE AND THE NEW TAX LAW

Several tax benefits long associated with real estate ownership have been curtailed or eliminated so that limited partnerships, REIT'S, and outright ownership must be judged on the money making merits of the project. Most notably there are changes in the depreciation deductions, interest deduction, losses and the elimination of capital gains treatment:

1. No more accelerated depreciation. A deducation for residential rental property can be taken over 27.5 years (1/27.5 of the investment each year). Non-residential real estate is depreciated over 31.5 years. Only this straight line depreciation is available.

2. Home mortgage interest (first and second) would be deductible but only up to the original purchase price plus home improvements. Specific exceptions would apply for home equity loans used for education, medical costs and home improvements. Deduction for consumer interest payments (i.e., for auto loans, credit cards, student loans, life insurance loans) would be eliminated. However, interest paid on loans used to finance investments would continue to be deductible in an amount equal to investment income.

The interest deduction restrictions are to be phased in over 5 years:

1987 deduct 65%
1988 deduct 40%
1989 deduct 20%
1990 deduct 10%
1991 deduct none

Any interest which is disallowed for a taxable year during the transitional period and carried forward may be allowed in a subsequent year but limited to investment income in excess of investment interest paid or incurred.

The current at-risk rules will apply to real estate activities. Thus, the deduction for losses will be limited to the amount which the taxpayer has:

(1) Invested in the activity,

(2) Borrowed with personal liability for investment in the activity, or

(3) Pledged to the activity.

3. Active management rental real estate investors are allowed to use up to $25,000 in losses as a deduction to offset other income. The allowance is phased out, if the taxpayer's AGI is $100,000 or more. The allowance is "zero," if AGI is $150,000.

4. No more capital gains treatment for profits on the sale of real estate. Instead profits will be taxed as ordinary income.

7

Secrets
of Money
Management #2:
The Pay Yourself First Budget

DID YOU EVER SEE a newborn fawn try to walk for the first time? Its spindly legs and uncertainty make it shaky, confused and weak. Pretty soon, it learns and becomes surefooted, strong and fast. It's no wonder that those of you at the younger end of the wealth-building years, that is, twenty-one to twenty-six, may be wobbly when it comes to budgeting. This is probably the first time you have spent your own money and set your own life-style. Meanwhile, the slightly older reader may have already made a rough peace with his or her life-style choices. You may always feel that it's difficult to make ends meet, but at least you've had some practice.

In either case it's time to follow the Pay Yourself First Budget, designed to free you from the frustration of always being "a little short," or "unable to save," or "disappointed by your standard of living." The Pay Yourself First budget is a very easy and even fun regimen to follow. Once you are on the path you will keep going, probably forever, to build up wealth from earnings. People in their early thirties have great expectations, particularly executives and professionals with high compensation. But material expectations can be dashed in the face of today's prices—$20,000 for a luxury car, $200,000 for a large home, $10,000 for a deluxe vacation. Where have all the benefits gone?

I know that most of you rejoice if your expenditures equal your income. How will I get you to cut down even further in order to save/invest?—By giving you a new view of budgeting, spending, and investing. Like dieting, budgeting only works for the short term if it means deprivation. You cannot go against the grain; you cannot delay satisfaction (buying that painting, taking that trip, or purchasing that Italian suit) for too long before it all seems worthless. At least I can't. So let's forget the ugly defeatist word *budget*. Yuck! What I want has nothing to do with budgeting; let's call it repositioning. I want you to 1) know what you spend; 2) know how you allocate your income in terms of percentages; 3) prioritize your spending in terms of satisfaction; and 4) reposition your low-priority expenditures toward investments.

DETERMINING PERCENTAGES

The program is designed to make you start spending the right way, the most enjoyable way, and the most satisfying way. The concept is so simple that it is practically revolutionary. First, don't focus on how *much* money you spend. Concentrate only on the *percentage* of your spendable income used for each type of expenditure. When the exercise is complete you will have a picture of your spending habits which looks like those pie diagrams that you studied in economics class—except that it will show *your* economic situation. Here's one for a hypothetical couple:

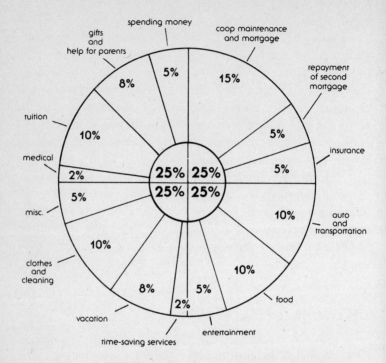

To get this quick-fix budget, first use the figures in the Income/Expense Sheet (pages 16–17). If you earn $30,000 per year and spend $5,000 in food, then ⅙ or 18 percent of your budget is spent on food.

Next, get more specific. Prepare your first and last detailed and verified expenditure list. Use check stubs, credit card receipts, and even keep a three-month diary if you spend cash haphazardly. Include *all* your income. After all, this is for you, not the IRS. Don't kid yourself. If you add to your expense account without reimbursement don't delude yourself into omitting that expenditure. Here is a sample list for a family with children.

Expenses	Fixed Expenses	Flexible Expenses	Spendable Income
SHELTER COSTS: Rent, heat, telephone, mortgage, electricity, maintenance, other utilities, taxes, snow removal, sanitation, gardening, swimming pool, other.			
SERVICES: Hair dressing, dry cleaning, transportation, professionals, tips, domestic help.			
FUN: Sports, entertainment, vacations, health club, country club, books, newspapers, pocket money, courses.			
DEBTS: Interest on personal loan, interest on credit card, other.			
NECESSITIES: Food, clothing, medical, pharmaceuticals.			
TAXES: Federal, state, local, gift, FICA/Social Security.			
INSURANCE: Disability, life, health, auto, home.			
CHILD RELATED EXPENSES: Education, child care.			
RELIGION & CHARITIES: Dues, contribution, literature, tithe.			
PAY YOURSELF FIRST: Investment, savings, pension/profit sharing, and other retirement planning.			

FIXED VS. FLEXIBLE EXPENSES

Next, categorize your expenses as fixed or flexible. You have discretion over the latter but not the former. Loans and shelter are the two most common fixed expenses. Can any others be reduced without pain? Even with fixed expenses, ask:

- If the expense is a loan payment—Should I refinance for a longer period of lower interest to reduce expenditures?
- If the expense is in shelter costs—Have I gone overboard in choosing my digs? (Shelter is usually calculated as 33 percent of spendable income in urban areas, and 25 percent elsewhere.)

Usually it is the flexible expenses that devour earnings. Prioritize; simply rank your expenditures as important, moderately important, and unimportant. Begin by eliminating the unimportant items. This in itself may be enough to begin a savings/investment plan satisfying to you. If not, eliminate some of the moderately important expenditures. Then Pay Yourself First! Don't just eliminate the amount, write out a check to a special account and start saving. The kind of account depends on how much you have. If you begin with $50 it must be a savings account; if you are retirement-minded, use an IRA until $2,000, the maximum contribution in any given year, is completed; if you have more available, invest in a money market fund or begin to purchase units in a mutual fund.

If necessary, send yourself a bill to pay yourself first. Place the bill in your filing system under "Unpaid Bills—Penalty." Make yourself as important as your creditors. You'll be amazed at how regularly you will be able to save and how the savings will soon become investments.

THE TIME/MONEY BALANCE SHEET

If you find that cutting down on spending is just not resulting in enough savings, I suggest you do a second listing of expenditures you make in order to save time. Many young people in a hurry spend a small fortune on time-saving services. Prepare a Time/Money balance sheet, which puts you in control of the money you spend in this way. Use it:

- To help you spend less money by eliminating services that do not save you time.
- To help you reduce anxiety about spending for services that do save you time.
- To help you judge what you should charge for your services.
- To help you judge the value of others' services to you.

In Column A, list the activities you hire others to do for you—our hypothetical couple's list includes restaurants, dry cleaners, gardening, taxis, directory assistance, accounting, house cleaning, hair dressing, and more.

In Column B enter the money you spend per week for the service (if the expense is monthly or yearly, divide by 4.3 or 52 respectively).

In Column C enter the time per week you saved by paying for the service (do not fool yourself).

In Column D enter your *Money/Time Ratio,* the figure you get by dividing the money spent by the time saved.

In Column E comment on the result:

1. Are you saving any time at all (i.e., when using directory assistance)?
2. Is it a good deal? A cheap way to save time (i.e., hair dressing)?
3. Are you getting pleasure as well, and therefore would like to keep up the service for other than time-saving reasons (i.e., eating out)?

Activity	Cost Per Week	Time Saved P/W	Money/ Time Ratio	Comments
Hair cutting	$10.00	3 hours	$3.30	
Eating out	$35.00	1 hour	$35.00	
House cleaning	$40.00	5 hours	$8.00	
Dry cleaning	$10.00	2 hours	$5.00	
Lawn mowing	$1.00	10 min. (.1 hr)	$6.00	
Gardening	$3.00	20 min. (.2 hr)	$9.00	
Taxis	$12.00	3 hours	$4.00	
Home repairs	$20.00	3 hours	$6.00	
Snow removal (leaf cleanup)	$1.00	20 min. (.2 hr)	$3.00	
Wallpapering	$1.00	10 min. (.1 hr)	$6.00	
Directory assistance	$5.00	0	*	
Accounting services	$5.00	20 min. (.2 hr)	$15.00	

4. Is the service one you need because you cannot do the activity yourself (i.e., accounting work; snow shoveling if you have a heart condition)?

READJUSTING THE PERCENTAGES

Keep adjusting the percentages in your pie chart for the better. Choose the percentage of your spendable income that you will use for savings, investments, and retirement. Reduce your nonfixed (flexible) expenses to accommodate your new, greater Pay Yourself First expenditure. If your fixed expenditures are so high that you can't make the adjustment you may have to renegotiate your loans for a longer period of payment, or consider a change of residence. This happens very infrequently. Sometimes just reducing your taxes is enough to adjust your expenditures and "find money" to Pay Yourself First.

Now for the best part. Three months after you begin to follow your Pay Yourself First Budget plan, redo your budget. Add something special—a fur coat, a new car, a trip. This may increase your fixed debt. But by eliminating your low-ranked expenditures you can "find" money to fulfill some dreams without eliminating savings or investment. Remember, old habits die hard—give yourself at least three months to readjust.

WHAT HAPPENS IF YOU AND YOUR PARTNER CAN'T AGREE ON PRIORITIES?

Naturally, since prioritizing is *the* priority in the Pay Yourself First Budget, things get pretty rough when you and your P.O.S.S.L.Q. (Person of the Opposite Sex Sharing the Same Living Quarters) don't agree.

Personal money management is a fascinating topic. Even more fascinating is learning how others manage their money. A couple's pattern of spending, saving, and otherwise using their two paychecks is often as private a matter as their sex life. Certainly they are all different but there are threads of similarity.

We've been led to believe that there is a new and increasing phenomenon called the "two-paycheck" family. Presumably this refers to the growing group of working couples that are either married or living together, with neither partner having primary responsibility for support of the family.

Of course, we have always had husbands and wives who both worked. But these were not considered a two-paycheck family. The woman's work was considered "extra" money, usually not to be used to support but to enhance. It wasn't long ago that working women would hide that fact since it was an embarrassment that their husbands could not fully support their families. This attitude is gone. But when traditional attitudes change, some very surprising replacements are found.

As a financial planner, I have counseled many two-paycheck families on the Pay Yourself First Budget. And I have seen that it is primarily differences in priorities that cause that little knot of hostility couples feel when they budget together. Ideally a compromise will be reached, but not until you sort out your type of imbalance.

The Breadwinner Syndrome

This strikes couples in which both work as well as those in which only one works. Frequently, regardless of who is earning more money in a two-paycheck family, one member emerges as the "breadwinner." Often a woman making slightly less or the same as her husband feels that she is the breadwinner, because her situation may be an unusual one and because she is taking on responsibilities greater than others around her. Many very successful women who are married have a secret resentment about being the breadwinner, while men rarely do. By the same token, when a woman goes into the work force for the first time after many years when there is already an established pattern of the husband having supported the family, he continues to have the feeling of breadwinnership regardless of her earnings and success.

Imbalance Resulting from the Way You Use Your Money

Often the partner whose money is used most visibly, for example, allocated for mortgage payments every month and furniture purchases rather than for everyday spending money, considers him or herself the "breadwinner" regardless of who is earning more. Trouble sometimes crops up when partners have two different philosophies. The one who is perceived as the breadwinner will usually prevail, and this can create resentment.

Which of You Is Really Earning Less?

There is a definite difference in the use and attitude toward the two paychecks when they are truly imbalanced. Unquestionably, the couple whose paychecks are equal have the easiest time of it. They will generally pool their money without concern about who owns what, they will buy things jointly with ease, and they will regard the other's money as their own since they have contributed an equal amount. Where there is true financial imbalance, money attitudes usually depend upon what I call "couple classification." Is the couple married or living together? Do they have children or are they childless? Is the woman a new entrant into the job market or one who began the relationship working? Is the couple conservative or risk taking, long-range or short-range planners, necessity buyers or luxury buyers? Depending on these classifications, imbalance of funds can mean more or less to them.

You must get a focus on your own brand of money-making decisions. Then you must listen (that's the hardest part) to the reasons for the other's priorities. Then you must judge which is more sensible in the relative scheme of things and who will suffer most if their priorities do not win out. Finally, look again at the prioritizing exercises and come up with a compromise list that allows for periodic review. In the end, for both of you to get what you want, you may need to borrow some money. This alternative will be explored in the next chapter.

8

Secrets
of Money
Management #3:
Debt Is Good, But Manage It Well

THE PROBLEM WITH THE AVERAGE INVESTOR'S use of credit, particularly those in the wealth-building years, is that they use it for the wrong things and at too high a price. in this chapter, we will explore the secrets of credit and provide you with a total reeducation, or perhaps a first education.

When you borrow money you pay for the privilege. This payment is called *interest*, and it is the flip side of the coin that you would receive if you bought bonds, mortgages, or any of the other many investments that are income-producing. You are now on the other side of the fence; your object is to borrow money at its cheapest possible rate. This means that you want to be as credit-worthy as possible so that you don't have to pay a premium to anyone because you are not considered a good risk. It also means that you want to be as creative as possible so that you can contrive ways of borrowing money at its cheapest. You also want to borrow for the right things so that you are not paying a premium because of the reason you're borrowing.

THE CREDIT CARD TRAP

In general the most expensive type of borrowing is for tangible consumer goods. In short, buying your refrigerator on credit or amassing purchases on credit cards that you don't pay back within a month are the most expensive ways to borrow. Do you realize how truly expensive it is? First, there is the interest charges itself—usually around 19 percent on credit cards and most consumer purchases. Second, you may be required to purchase a certain amount of product to be given the privilege of borrowing in the first place. Retailers mark up their prices because *they* are charged 5 to 10 percent of the purchase price if they permit a customer to use the credit card. Just as there has been a tremendous surge in the past decade in the use of credit cards, we may see an equal decline in the next ten years—because merchants themselves cannot afford to give to the credit card companies the required percentage of the purchase price.

Even at 19 percent, young people use credit cards with too much aplomb. There are some logical reasons for this, of course. The average young person doesn't have enough money to start a new home or get a wardrobe for work. The whole purpose of this book is to help readers without a great job, an inheritance, or a winning lottery ticket to make their way. But they do need things. In fact, at the beginning they need things more than investments, because they must invest in themselves. You must have the proper suit or you can't interview. You must have the proper chair in your home or you can't sit. Nor is it wise in these inflationary times to buy junk for temporary purposes. How else can you purchase without a credit card and the high interest that it brings?

This will be a matter of personality and life-style more than it will be of financial planning. However, to a financial planner certain suggestions are clear. First and foremost, while it may be hard to accept and it may not be true of everyone, most of you will purchase things that they will no longer want within a two-year period. By this I mean your style of dressing, your taste in furniture, your taste in vacations and other material goods will change rapidly in the first two to five years after beginning to work. People come from high school and college with group tastes and with the tastes of their parents; they have not yet developed their individual tastes. Therefore, you should give some extra thought to whether you are buying the right things. Chances are, you probably have a temporary love affair with your new suit, your new car, and your new art collection. You will gain more exposure to the world and you will change your mind. Your clothing needs will change as you gain the higher levels of career and employment.

This means that you should buy with a temporary thought in mind for a short period of time. Do not buy expensive. In fact, as revolutionary as it might sound, if you can rent do so. If you would like a big-screen TV and you feel you deserve that as your gift to yourself from your first six months of paychecks, see if you can rent it instead. Make sure that you are renting without a service charge or a charge that's really the equivalent of interest. Naturally you're going to have to compare the cost of large purchase items with the renting of them. By and large, though, you will find that in your temporary status (up to two years after beginning to work) you are probably better off without the high interest rates and without actually owning an item. Don't forget, one of the better things about interest rates is that they are deductible from income; but while your income is low, that deduction is not useful to you.

Of course, you can't rent clothes (except for furs and jewelry; I've been fascinated by my super-wealthy clients who do not buy those furs and jewelry that you think they own—they rent them. But that's for another book on "Cheating By the Rich and Famous."). For now, dress in the way you like; have fun with your clothing but unless you're absolutely sure of yourself and your taste, don't start to invest in dress quite yet.

A $300 suit may not be worth it in a year when it's not the kind of style that you want to project.

Still, you're going to need to use credit for some of your purchases and you're going to want to own others. Begin by going back to the last chapter, on the Pay Yourself First Budget. It is here that you can make sure that your expenditures don't exceed your income. It is here that you can pace (there's that important word again) your spending habits. Ease into your new job during the first six months and learn what you have left over. Use the Pay Yourself First Budget to ensure that you are using your money for your priorities. Even if you end up with nothing left over, let the discretionary funds be spent on purchases you really want. The greatest problem of American spenders is that they do not know what they spent their money on. It is never the individual who has bought art, even clothing or a vacation who is the overspender. It is people who have spent so many dollars in restaurants, transportation, and other things that they cannot pindown who become the overspenders. This is because they have lost control over their spending, they have not focused on a budget and they don't have a sense of what they are getting for their hard-earned dollars. In fact, it is never the investment, win or lose, or the important item of expense that will do you in. It is the day-to-day, self-imposed losses that you suffer because you are not aware of how you are dealing with the little expenses in life. The Pay Yourself First Budget will do it for you by giving you a framework and making sure you use your discretionary money *first* to buy what you want. Later, when you have enough things actually to get on with your life, that Pay Yourself First money will go into your investments.

Naturally you may not have enough to start up your new adult life-style without borrowing. If that is true, please don't use credit cards. In fact, if they weren't so darn convenient I would tell you to throw them out all together or not accept them. For you will be solicited again and again by store credit cards and major credit card companies. The convenience is fantastic. If you learn to pay your credit card every single month and actually incur no charge on it, it becomes a great boon. If you become a traveler, it will help you overseas, should you be in a really tight spot. If you have investments for thirty days, you can use your credit card so that you can keep your investments intact and not have to pull out any money to pay bills during this time. Instead of having money in no-interest checking accounts, credit cards can be used. But remember you can get into big trouble because long after the consumer good has been used up or discarded, the credit cost will linger on.

BORROWING FROM THE BANK

To establish credit wisely, don't use a credit card, use your bank. In Chapter 12, on establishing a relationship with a professional, I tell you how to use a bank and how important it is to have a banking relationship. I often tell my younger people the most important service that our office can give is to get them a relationship with a good bank. Start immediately. First, try to get a personal loan from a bank. The interest rates are still high; a noncollateralized personal consumer loan is the highest banking rate that you'll find. Nevertheless, it is considerably lower than anything you'll get on a credit card, by a minimum of two points if not more. Next, should you already be in trouble with your credit cards, you might get what's called a consolidation loan: one loan from a bank that helps you pay off all your credit cards and reduces your interest rate. Most banks will give small consumer loans to a young person with a good steady job. If for some reason you can't get such a loan, your next step must be to get some money into that bank and open up a savings account. From that you will take a passbook loan for the amount of money that you have. No bank will turn down a borrower who has an account with them if all they want to borrow is the same amount of money they already have in the account. They merely freeze the account, let it grow at whatever interest rate it is deposited at, and lend you the money to buy your items. You may ask, isn't it cheaper to use my cash, wipe out my account, and take no loan? Yes, it is cheaper but not smarter. You need to develop credit, and this is the first step. Once you have established credit, you have also established your banking relationship—two financial birds with one stone.

The next step is to make sure you pay that loan on time, without incurring any late or service charges. Use your filing system to keep records of payments and when payments are due. Again, you are beginning a lifelong habit of paying those bills where service charges can be incurred or where credit ratings can suffer if payments are not made on time. Meanwhile, use the money wisely and make sure your Pay Yourself First Budget is revised to show the monthly payments that must be made. Throughout the last fifty years, interest rates on borrowing inevitably have gone up. You may find that money borrowed three or four years earlier is the best money you ever borrowed because the interest rate was so low. You'll also find that if you go the passbook method you will have a considerably smaller amount of interest to pay than with a regular consumer loan, and perhaps 7 percent less than a credit card loan. Young people often ask me what they should do with their graduation gift of $1,000 or $2,000—they'd like to know whether they should invest it. My answer is "Yes, invest in credit." Open up a bank account with that money and then borrow it. Use the borrowed money for your investments. It's the greatest learning experience in the world.

WEALTH BUILDING THROUGH CREDIT

As you earn more, get older and become more sophisticated, your credit needs will broaden. And here is perhaps the essence of what can be taught to the younger person. *Learn to use credit to build wealth.* Anyone of you who goes through the forms in this book—the Pay Yourself First Budget, the repositioning of assets—and learns how to use the chapter on the chemistry of investments will do well. But what's going to separate those of you who become wealthy from those of you who are merely "comfortable" will not be investment brilliance as much as it will be understanding and using credit to build wealth. And you do not need to know much about credit; what you need to do is make an attitude adjustment, a change in your way of thinking and in what you have been taught.

There is no virtue, none whatsoever (no matter what your mother told you), in using your own cash for investments. If you could get 100 percent financing on an investment, take it. Let's say you have saved $5,000 and would like to make an investment in real estate. Except for public limited partnerships (discussed on page 158), there probably is no investment you could possibly make. On the other hand, let's say someone has an apartment in co-op ownership worth $55,000. If they were willing to take your $5,000 as a down payment and transfer to you the ownership of their co-op with an agreement that you would pay them $50,000 slowly, over time at a particular interest rate, this allows you to buy. So one fundamental purpose of financing, particularly for the younger person, is to make up for the cash that you do not have.

Now take the same concept a step further. Let's say you had the $55,000, in cash, to pay for that co-op. If you paid for it in cash, you might be able to make a deal for a better price and pay perhaps, $50,000, saving $5,000 on the purchase price. If the co-op appreciated in value by 10 percent (a not unreasonable yearly appreciation, even in a modest location) it would be worth and you could sell it for $60,500 at the end of a year. If you paid cash, you would have made $10,500 on a $50,000 investment; in other words, 21 percent increase on your money. However, if you had financing and used only $5,000 of your own cash, you would have made the same $10,500 on a $5,000 investment. In other words, you would have earned over 200 percent on your money. You can't get that anywhere. That's the importance of leveraging. The same investment, the same risks, and a startlingly different return.

The usual argument of young people when they hear this example is that they can't afford to carry a loan for the remaining $50,000. If that is the case, then buy something cheaper that is leveraged. Use your Pay Yourself First Budget to learn what you really can afford. Let me give you some Dutch uncle advice: most young people underestimate their ability to earn and to carry debt. If you cut out the 19 percent interest that you are paying on your credit cards, you will be able to carry a substantial amount of debt at 11 to 12 percent over a long term, for real estate or other types of investments.

By no means is real estate the only type of investment that could and should be leveraged. Stocks are another. Rather than engaging in the more risky purchasing of options (puts and calls), consider buying some stock on margin. Remember you are taking a loan. Stock is not a favorite investment for buying on credit but you can buy up to 50 percent of certain stocks on credit alone. If you feel strong enough in the market to take that chance, go to it. Most young people do not have the expertise for stock trading. But if you do, think leverage in this area as well as in every other investment you can find.

For some investments you must self-leverage. By this I mean that you must take out a loan (perhaps a personal loan) because the investment does not come with its own financing. The big advantage with real estate and even stock is that there is financing available through banks or through the seller. Some investments you may find do not have this aspect to them. If it's worth owning, it is usually worth borrowing to buy. The best kind of investment leveraging is far and away that of real estate. Without repeating the material already set forth in Chapter 6, let me remind you that the beauty of real estate is that it can be income-producing. This means that, properly bought, real estate will pay its own interest and principle by yielding rental income to you. The perfect piece of real estate is one where the rental income to you plus the tax savings that you will get equal or exceed the carrying costs of the real estate. These carrying costs include the interest rates.

CREATIVE FINANCING

Creative financing is very important for the younger purchaser, because he or she may not even have the basic down payments necessary to get credit in the first place. For a bank to find you credit-worthy, no more than 36 percent of your income should go for the payment of interest from all loans (debt service), maintenance for housing, land taxes and any other costs of shelter. Of the 36 percent banks like to see only 25 percent or so going toward the cost of housing. This is not a rule of thumb that you need live by, but it's at least some indication for new people starting out who like to have some rules.

Once again, creative financing is best and most easily found in real estate. This may be because real estate is traditionally the most leveraged of all investments. Look back to Chapter 3 and read the characteristics of investments to see which are most easily leveraged and which cannot be leveraged at all. In real estate you have two people interested in making a deal, the buyer and the seller (often the broker is a third), and so all kinds of creative financing is available. Only the human imagination and the law of contracts can limit financing creativity. Some examples are:

1. The buyer taking back a second mortgage or even a first mortgage where a bank will not give sufficient funds to purchase.
2. Split funding, in which both the buyer and seller become obligated under a mortgage to a bank, with the buyer agreeing to hold the seller harmless for his share and then agreeing to pay off the entire mortgage amount within a short period of time after they have established a credit record.

3. The broker waiting for his commission so that the original loan can be taken sans brokerage fees.
4. The vast variety of mortgages available on the market today (see page 145).
5. Equity sharing—a partnership between parent and adult child to purchase real estate.

The individual who is the most creative with regard to financing wins. Frequently you will hear of young people becoming millionaires well before the age of thirty without any seeming background in personal finance or investments. Occasionally this will be because of special abilities such as the invention of a computer game, stardom, or even winning the lottery. But there are many quiet young millionaires out there. Usually they have done it not because their investments were so brilliant or so unusual but because their financing ability was so great.

For example, one young couple purchased six apartment houses in the first eight years of their marriage. By the time they were thirty, they had both quit their jobs (which, incidentally, they had prepared for by going to college and seriously believed they were going to pursue lifelong). The apartment ownership was just too lucrative. How did it happen? They had heard that there was money to be made in real estate but could not afford their own home. On the other hand, they were able to afford an apartment house in a relatively modest area of New Jersey. Since the rent from the apartment house would pay its own carrying costs, they purchased it and discovered that within eighteen months it had gone up in value. They borrowed against that piece of real estate, just enough to buy a second apartment house. The rental was actually slightly less than the carrying needs, but the excess rent from the first apartment house made up for it. The third time they bought an apartment house, it hit big. The neighborhood was rising and condominium conversion was growing. They converted their apartment house to a condominium. Because of their lack of know-how, it took them three and one-half years to do what is normally done in one year. But when it was complete and all the apartments sold, they had made a substantial profit. They bought another apartment house, this time in a high-rent area with rents that far exeed the carrying costs. They began to realize they might be able to retire from their jobs and work at being landlords instead. To do this they needed a piece of property that produced a great deal more income and less appreciation. Even real estate moguls can't eat appreciation. They put out the word to every broker in the area: they were interested in a high income-producing commercial property at *any* price. They were bombarded within six months with forty potential properties, and quit their jobs to investigate every one. Three were chosen. The couple made separate financing deals with every single seller. One property that they particularly wanted they could not afford at all. Even creative financing would not work. Instead, they offered the seller a part of the business profits. The seller accepted and became the junior partner in his own enterprise. This does take talent, guts, and of course at least normal luck. It also takes the important ingredient of listening to the other guy and trying to understand what makes him tick and what will make him make a deal.

FINAL THOUGHTS ON
WHAT MAY BE HOLDING YOU BACK

The first enduring problem is that most young people are burdened by their parents' view of credit. During the Depression, credit was a very dangerous thing if you did not know how to use it. You probably could not pay back your interest and therefore might lose whatever collateral you put up. Buying on margin and buying stocks on credit made many a suicide out of a millionaire. Parties to celebrate the end of a thirty-year mortgage were the norm. Today most home owners renew their mortgages because the equity has grown enough and they know that it is a mistake to keep such important assets illiquid. Your philosophy of credit must change with the times.

The other area relating to credit that deeply disturbs many young people is the student loan. Whether one goes into bankruptcy to try to discharge these loans or one dutifully pays them over the first ten years of one's work life also depends on one's philosophy of credit. Remember first that the student loan is something that does help you establish your credit once it is paid. Remember too that the government is a lousy collection agency. They neither like nor are fully equipped to collect unpaid debt. The result is that there is no way that you can make a better deal faster and more often than with your student loan. If you cannot pay or if you're killing your Pay Yourself First Budget and giving yourself no leeway to save and invest, make a deal. To do so call your State Higher Education loan officer.

Any of you who are still in the midst of your education should read my book *Your Kids, Your Money*, if only for the chapters regarding paying for college. Many burdens can be alleviated. You might talk to your parents about borrowing. For example, borrowing against an insurance policy is sometimes cheaper than the costs of the student loan. If your parents were to borrow the money and have you pay them back, they would not only get a tax deduction, which they might very well be able to use better than you, but you might be paying back at a lower rate. I say "might" because student loans are generally one of the best deals in town.

Which comes to our last word of warning regarding credit. Do your best not to lend or borrow from family members unless it's part of an organized tax-saving program. When Shakespeare said "Neither a borrower nor a lender be," he did not mean banks and other institutions, but rather friends and family. It is a bad mistake to become embroiled and rely on credit largesse from friends and family and even, as hard-hearted as it sounds, to give any. An attorney I knew years ago used to say "I wonder why he is so mad at me, I never did anything for him." I believe that says it all when it comes to family and friends.

9

Secrets
of Money
Management #4:
Changing Your Perceptions about
Money and Learning to
Take a Chance

I THINK YOU'LL UNDERSTAND THIS CHAPTER best if you understand its evolution. Originally it was going to be devoted to certain highly aggressive growth investments—options trading, rare coins, and new company stocks. My point was to familiarize you with risky investments that could show a big payoff. After your conservative planning was underway, I wanted to make sure that every once in a while you'd try a risky, let's-go-for-broke investment that might make you really rich (or really sorry), but would be exciting enough to keep you interested in the money world around you.

I wanted you to be brave about investing; to see opportunities and to seize them. I knew that if you did this on a regular basis, you would eventually be very rich. Unfortunately, as I began to write about my three chosen aggressive investments I realized that just knowing about them wouldn't do the trick. I had to help you *believe* differently about money, be less afraid to lose it, be more receptive to trying new things. This is your time to experiment with money.

Remember that you have already structured your money habits in a careful, almost plodding fashion. My Pay Yourself First Budget, goals program, investment characteristics analysis, and more make anything really fatal (bankruptcy, poverty) impossible. With some of that pay-yourself money, or profit from other investments, or gifts and inheritance, you should take a chance. This is the time to lose, if necessary. More important, this is your chance to restructure your money belief system so that you react differently to all types of money opportunities as they arise. Whenever you judge an investment, choose a job, buy furniture, even find a penny, your money belief system comes into play. It's our *philosophy* of money that ultimately dictates whether we will do just okay, or be very rich indeed.

To get you into a "wealthy" frame of mind, there are some concrete exercises you can do—and I suggest you begin to do them on faith. This may seem silly, but I'm dead serious. *These exercises work for everyone.* They are a combination of what I have learned from positive thinkers, money managers, high-powered executives, and even spiritualists. I suggest that if you need to work on your philosophy of money—if money matters really scare you, bore you, or worry you—that you read as much as you can about positive thinking in general.

If you visit a religious or spiritual bookstore you'll be surprised to find the number of books written about money—not about its evil, but about its good. The fear of losing, of being poor or struggling forever, is to forget how really rich we are, even without money. Lighten up about money! You'll then be more flexible and able to invest, try new things, get what you want. The nervous, picky, plodding ones will never make it. I'd like to shake the worry out of you, but I can't.

Most people believe that to be rich one needs luck, opportunity, and brilliance in some combination. Which one do you think is the most important? In any case, you probably don't think you have any of them. So long as you don't, you won't! I know a number of millionaires and while there are many roads to success each found his or her share of the above three factors. Can you really learn to be lucky? Can you create opportunity? Can you become a genius? Yes, yes, yes. Incredible as it seems, I can give you exercises for achieving each. But there is one leap of faith that you must take, one thing I cannot teach. You must believe the following: your money situation is *entirely* in your power. The knowledge of your power in this area puts you in control—you'll never be too scared to decide, act, and profit; you'll see the truth from the flim-flam; most important, you'll do what you want with your life because money won't be a constraint.

If you accept your power and your control, you'll realize the importance of the three basic exercises I will outline for you now. Some of you may have heard of these programs, to others they may be brand new. If practiced regularly they change your way of responding and therefore change your life.

HOW TO GET LUCKY—USING THE AFFIRMATION

An affirmation is a positive statement that when repeated frequently comes true. For example: "Every day in every way I'm getting better and better." Much has been written about affirmations; nevertheless, no matter how analytically they are explained there is something mystical about them. Here are some exercises. You must actually write or say them out loud—and please do it, even if it's just to humor me; you'll be so astonished at the effect that you'll think you're creating your own luck.

Sample Affirmations to Say Every Day

These are examples of some people's affirmations. Choose your own after reminding yourself of your goals.

By March 15, 19____, I will have a $100 a week raise.

In 60 days my gross receipts will be $2,500 a week.

I will increase my investment growth by 20 percent per year in the coming year.

By this time next year, I will own my own home.

An opportunity to make $10,000 in profit will come my way by next month.

I will sell my used car at a profit by mid-summer.

Next write or say why you really don't think that your affirmations will materialize. Here are some common reasons for negativity.

Negative Affirmations

This whole thing is dumb.

I'm not lucky enough.

I'm not smart enough.

The car isn't worth the money.

$10,000 is too good to be true.

I'm not good enough to get such a big raise.

Then negate the negatives.

Reaffirmations

This is a unique and intelligent way to get lucky.

I'm a lucky person and I can do it.

I'm a smart person and I can do it.

This car is worth the money since new cars are so expensive.

$10,000 is a fair and just profit for my risk.

I'm a good worker and deserve a raise.

You can try many affirmations; you will find they work. How can just writing or saying good things and negating negative thoughts make you lucky? I'm not quite sure, but some or all of these factors might be involved: action follows belief; you may inspire others to help you; your desires become specific and therefore they can be fulfilled.

I once had a large and beautiful house to sell. It had been on the market since November and it was now March, and I needed the money to buy another house in April. I was pretty scared. I learned about affirmation at this time and believed that I must be desperate to try such a silly thing. But I did it. Every day for one week I said, "I'll sell my house and get the full price." I started on Monday, and by Saturday I was drinking champagne toasts with my husband, for we had indeed sold the house at full price. Saying the affirmation had made me realize how very important the sale was to me. I made selling a life priority. I called the brokers, greeted every potential buyer with enthusiasm. Since I liked the house and found it hard to give up, I had virtually avoided the past buyers and let the broker do all the talking. Also, I confided the affirmation to my husband, and he got on the band wagon and he showed how our swimming pool operated—a fascinating lure in the dreary month of March. Most important, the affirmation established it as a priority, and priorities get done.

It often seems like luck is involved too. Let me tell you how I got my full purchase price and you'll see how we control our own "luck."

The buyers offered $5,000 less than our price. Still an acceptable deal. But my affirmation said *full* price, and I was determined to get it. I counteroffered with full price, but I'd leave the curtains and fixtures. They accepted. *But*, the curtains and fixtures were actually worth about $10,000. Had I been thinking right I would have offered them in exchange for *more* than my asking price. Oddly enough, because I transact so much real estate and because my experience dictates that the seller gets something less than the asking price, I never thought to extend my demands and my luck. In the end I got just what I affirmed, no more, no less. I missed an opportunity to make more profit.

HOW TO RECOGNIZE AND SEIZE OPPORTUNITIES— USING VISUALIZATION AND TREASURE MAPPING

Most people don't get what they want because they don't have the slightest idea of what it is. Every time I do a radio show I ask the listeners to close their eyes and visualize someone they respect congratulating them for a financial success: "Congratulations, you have just _____." You fill in the blank. Visualize the opportunity you want—you got a new job, bought your first apartment, bought your first stock. This is all part of goal setting, but it is not enough. You must next be superspecific. The more of a novice you are with money, the more specific you must be. What industry stock, how many shares, what price-earning ratio, when do you want your profit taken?

Treasure mapping is an arts-and-crafts game in which you actually draw or paste up a picture of what you want to achieve. Again, real estate brought me to treasure mapping. I was looking at an apartment at the fashionable San Remo in Manhattan. I opened a closet door and found a door-sized treasure map pasted to the inside. "What's this?" I asked the seller (a multimillionaire, by the way). "It's my treasure map. I use it to visualize my next art purchase. I paste up exactly what I want and when I go to auction, I don't compromise. If it's not there I find it. I do it in business too. Some executives call it planning, some call it projections; to me it's visualizing the goal."

The millionaire's map was huge—the size of a closet door. It was labeled "Treasure Map," and it looked like a beautiful children's book illustration, with blue water and lines taking a winding path from a starting point to finish line. It reminded me of the Candy Land board game. Along the route were pictures of art treasures taken with a camera and cut from magazines. Next to each was marked the date and place of an auction.

Since then I have seen many treasure maps. One woman whose goal was to lose weight simply pasted a pinup of models with her proportions and body type (only thinner and in good shape) all over the house. And she had pasted her own face over the models'. Instant visualization! I've done my own treasure maps with furniture and houses.

If it's a tangible item you crave, treasure mapping is great. You could (and should) prepare a net worth statement that you would *like* to have. Visualize yourself with the wealth, security, and cash flow you want. Write it up as if it were already so. Then go make it happen!

Every opportunity you long for is out there. The more clearly you are focused, the more directed you are, the easier it will be to recognize and seize the opportunity. Once you have it, of course, you must know what to do next. Do you finance the house, buy it outright, pay off a loan fast or slow, take the vacation, or buy the bonds—a conflict of opportunities. It takes a little acquired brilliance to figure this out.

HOW TO ACQUIRE BRILLIANCE—USING COGNETICS

Cognetics is a thinking discipline developed by an Australian, Count Michael de Saint-Arnaud. Today it is used by executives of major corporations to reprogram their methods of thinking, refresh creativity, and enhance business success. You can use it to think smarter. Specifically, when it comes to money, Count Michael suggests you change your "perceptual idiom"—the way you think about money and property. In an interview with me he gave the following suggestions.

Let me give you an example of what I mean by a *perceptual idiom*. My aunt has owned hair salons in Melbourne for many years. She once told me that the first thing she notices about a person is that person's hair. It makes sense that a hairdresser's perceptual idiom (habit of noticing) would be hair. I am a cognitive scientist. I have a tendency to notice the way a person does his thinking.

I'm sure it wouldn't shock you to hear that artists notice art, that lawyers think legally, that dancers like to dance, etc. So, it comes as no surprise that prosperous people tend to notice the opportunities that exist in a situation. In other words, they are receptive to prosperity. Be receptive!

The most important point that can be made about prosperity thinking is this: *if you want to be ten times more prosperous, then you must have a perceptual idiom that causes you to think ten times more prosperously.*

How to begin to think more prosperously is what cognetic exercises are all about. Saint-Arnaud explains as follows:

> Simply stated, the brain works as a patterning system. It builds up patterns of experience (through repetition) and these patterns actually *store thinking.* Once the pattern is triggered off, either by outside stimulus or on command, all the information stored in the pattern can be immediately put out. This is useful for living and saves us the trouble, for example, of having to re-invent breakfast every morning! Once you build up the pattern of "breakfast" you can store that information for daily use when you get hungry in the morning. Other patterns may be simpler or more complicated but basically work the same way.
>
> For example: If I trigger off the pattern with the word "kangaroo," notice the information that, for you, is released. I say "for you" because it does vary with individual experience. In my case, I've played with kangaroos and so that experience is also stored under the trigger "kangaroo." Let's try another one. Notice what happens in your brain's computer when we enter the word "repetition." What is coming up for you? If you are in sports or gym work it will mean one thing; if you are a copy editor, it will mean something else. Let's try the word "demulcent." Now notice what the brain is doing. Most brains do not have this information available so the tendency is

either to report "does not compute," or to come up with a *suggestion* (literally, information that is suggested from the brain's experiences files by the trigger command). The different response may be influenced by one's previous programming or whether one favors left or right brain operations. By the way, if you look up "demulcent" in the dictionary you will find "soothing." Last one: enter "coke." This is interesting because it is a nice example of how a pattern can be changed by repetition. "Coke" used to bring up "fuel," but today, for most people, up will come "drink" or "drug." This may give some simple insight into the brain as a patterning system.

Now you are ready to receive a new program for your brain. This is an executive program, a higher-order information processor called COS (cognetics operating system). Don't worry about this if you find it difficult. You don't need to understand it to make it work. You also don't *need* to know that the scientific description of what this program does for your brain is called S.N.C.M. —Stochastic Neuro-binary Cybernetic Meta-cognition.

This is what you *do* need to know. The *First Law of Cognetics* is that the Current View of the Situation can never be equal to the Better View of the Situation. This is written more conveniently as: CVS ≠ BVS. Repeat this to yourself two or three times until you are sure you understand it and can embrace it.

Now for the *Second Law of Cognetics*. The BVS is *ten times* the CVS, or, BVS = 10 × CVS. This law is important because it is one of measurement. Although all measurement is arbitrary, it gives structure and substance to what otherwise can be elaborate philosophical word games of the angels-on-the-heads-of-pins variety. So if the CVS is one unit, then a BVS could be ten units. If a CVS is on one level, then a BVS could be on a level ten times greater; etc. Since the most difficult feat in thinking is to escape from your own viewpoint, CVS to BVS can give you a way out.

Now the *Third Law of Cognetics*. Repeat "CVS to BVS" one hundred times a day. This will simply trigger the thought that your current view of the situation (any situation) is fine, but there is a much better view (ten times better) if only you care to notice it. That's all. This, to me, is the most important law because it converts cognetics from theory into practice. This law makes cognetics *actually work!* I suggest to you, as I do to others, that you try it for yourself for ten days. If it works, it will become intelligent behavior for you to continue using this program. If it doesn't, then you won't bother. A simple way of explaining how this trigger "CVS to BVS" works is to remind you about "kangaroo" or "coke" or my aunt, the hairdresser. That which is repeated builds into a pattern. Eventually, if the pattern is repeated often enough (which takes several years), it becomes a perceptual idiom. You have your current perceptual idiom. You could, of course, have one that is *ten times better*. The choice is yours.

Here is one last test to help you actually change your perceptions. Try this experiment: look around the room for red objects. (Don't read on until you've done so.) Now close your eyes and ask yourself how many *green* objects there are. Look again. Surprised? It was your focused attention on red that kept you from noticing things of another color.

The same applies to your perceptual idiom. If you focus your attention habitually on the bottle as half empty, you cannot notice that it is also half full. While your attention is on defending your CVS, you cannot be looking for a BVS. Simple but powerful. Cognetics is already being used at the highest levels of corporate, government, and scientific sectors. Now you can use it, too. The repetition each day is critical if you want it to become a habit.

THE FINAL EXERCISE

Finally, to be aggressive and right in your money decisions during your wealth-building years, *do something—anything— make a start*. Take with you luck (created by affirming your wishes); opportunity (created by defining your wishes); and brilliance (created by cognetics practice), so that you can re-think and thereby improve your situation.

Try this as your final mental exercise. Take $1,000 and affirm: What I most want out of this $1,000 is _____ (a new suit, an investment that gets me $2,000 in one year, art, coins, two weeks off, etc.).

Visualize with precision the goal.

Think about a new situation that allows you to reach the goal (perhaps you will rent the suit and keep the $1,000; perhaps you will borrow for the vacation; perhaps you will open a margin account for $1,000, buying $2,000 worth of stock and buying $10,000 worth on margin). But do *something* and learn to be receptive. It's the best lesson in the context of an overall conservative investment plan.

ONE YEAR LATER . . .

You have now learned to see things differently, make your own luck, and be specific with regard to your goals. If you have done all this correctly, it should have taken you about a year to really change your money thinking and your money habits. Now look back over the past year. What were the money opportunities you had and did not take? What opportunities could you have created but did not bother to create? What opportunities did you embrace? What were the outcomes?

By answering these questions you have focused on what you've been doing while you've been changing your money attitudes. Slowly you have been learning how to select invest-ments for the goals you have set. By now you have probably learned how to set those goals in the first place. You should have learned not to be frightened or fearful that there are no real opportunities for you. How can you now relate your new habits to the possibility of taking a chance and making signifi-cant money?

Let's take a real-life situation and see how setting goals, thinking broadly, and creating opportunity works. Today I received a brochure from a colleague of mine who is also an attorney. It simply stated, "Here is some information on a company in which I am involved." On the same day, I received six other brochures on all different kinds of investments; I also had my usual work to do, not to mention the completion of this book. I am also happily preparing for vacation and I started my child on his first day of school. Before I trained myself to look at everything that comes across my desk, I would have done one of two things with this prospectus—either left it in the pile of "to be done" and perhaps never got around to it, or just thrown it out. Either way I would have been passing up a valuable opportunity.

But I no longer do this. I now at least look at everything on my desk. The more I do this the faster I can spot what's important. Then right before I decide whether it is worth pursuing further, I think again. If I decide not to pursue it, I still use cognetics to see if I can look at the proposition in a different way, so that it will fit into my needs in the first place.

At present I have heavy investments in real estate. I could use either liquid assets, income-producing assets, or a speculation that might bring a quick return. Naturally, I am sophisticated enough to at least know my goals. If I didn't, I would use my affirmations and my treasure-mapping techniques to see if the investment put before me was the type that I really need. If it wasn't, however, I wouldn't stop there. I would use cognetics to see if that investment could be changed in some way—if it could be bettered to fit precisely into my needs.

For example, maybe the prospectus offers the sale of stocks plus a stock warrant for a dollar a share, with 500 shares as the minimum unit. The investment is in a new corporation organized a year ago in New York to purchase, own, race, and breed standard-bred horses. There is no question that this is a high-risk investment; however, millions have been made and it could be an opportunity. Does this fit into my needs? It does only if I analyze it to have enough potential for quick growth to balance my present illiquid position. In reading through the prospectus carefully I find that while there is a good, solid group backing this investment, potential for any real growth is several years away.

Before I toss the investment, though, I re-think the situation.

First, of course, I could take a small plunge rather than a major one. Second, I have other relationships with the fellow who suggested the investment. I could possibly purchase, say, 5000 shares by assigning over to him my rights in another investment that we hold together, which is at the moment illiquid. This is seeing the same situation in a slightly different light. Instead of using cash to take this risk, I can use other assets that are not available to me for any other purpose. Since he's very interested in having me buying this investment, he might help me in loosening up some of the cash tied up in another venture.

In the end I might very well take a risk I would have never considered otherwise. I've made an opportunity by not throwing out as "garbage" a prospectus on a new potential investment. I have seen the investment for what it is. It is not the get-rich-quick-overnight investment into which I should push every dollar; it has potential and problems, both of which I must deal with in a nonemotional way. And finally, although I really cannot afford to tie up additional funds, by rethinking the situation I find that I am able to make the purchase with funds that could not be used for any other purpose at the time.

10

What
Retirement
Means to You Now

Do you think it will never happen?—Retirement, I
mean. Well, you're wrong, and moreover it's likely that your
job or business will be the vehicle to provide for retirement.
It's not necessary to start very early—since we can't know the
future, it's wiser to invest for a twenty-five-year period with a
plan, rather than for a forty-year period haphazardly. In short,
you should seriously begin a full-fledged retirement program
between the ages of thirty-five and forty.

Meanwhile, there is one vital *must* even for the twenty-one
to thirty-five-year-old—an IRA, or Individual Retirement Account. This is available to all United States taxpayers, working
or married to someone working. With almost no effort it permits
you to build big retirement funds (especially if you start early,
like at the age of twenty). You can save up to $2,000 per year
or 100 percent of your income, whichever is smaller, in a designated fund in which: 1) the interest earned is not included in
your income tax in the year earned; and 2) the $2,000 is itself
deducted from your income in the year saved under certain
conditions. When you retire you can use the money and report
as income the amount withdrawn.

The IRA is a national benefit to encourage working people
to save for retirement. However, very few people understand
the rules.

198

My goal in this chapter is to impress upon you how much can actually be yours if you put your money into an IRA each year. You still might not realize how easily money grows over time. Reread Chapter 2 on time and money, take a good look at some of the figures, and add to them the boon that IRA money compounds *tax free* and may be tax deductible in the year of contributions.

How much money will you have at retirement from only $2,000 invested on January 1 of each year? If you get 10 percent interest, which is reasonable today, you'll have $361,886 in thirty years. Just to show the big difference a little time can make, let's compare this to what happens in thirty years at 10 percent if you make the IRA deposit on April 15 instead of January 1. You get only $319,548—a loss of $40,000. Still, this is not bad. But you must start now. If you wake up to this investment at age forty-five (like most Americans), at age sixty-five you'll have only $126,005 from January 1 contributions and $109,989 from April 15 contributions. *Not* enough to retire.

Here are the rules:

1. You may take a deduction even if you don't itemize.
2. You may not start withdrawing from the account until you reach age fifty-nine and a half, or become disabled.
3. You must start withdrawing from the account by age seventy and a half, and contributions after age seventy and a half are not deductible.
4. What you deduct from IRAs is fully taxed as ordinary income.
5. Unauthorized contributions and distributions are subject to penalties.
6. Deductible contributions must be based on payments received for rendering personal services, such as salary, wages, commissions, tips, fees, bonuses, or self-employed earned income.

There are four types of IRA plans—individual accounts, IRA annuities, IRA savings bonds, and employer plans. Most people choose the first. In any case you must open the account for the first time any time before you file the tax return for which you wish to take a deduction. Beyond that, you do not need any IRS approval to set up an IRA account. Companies such as banks, brokerage firms, and insurance companies offering IRA investment plans will provide all the necessary forms.

THE IRA ACCOUNT

An IRA account may be set up with a bank, savings and loan association, federally insured credit union, or other qualified trustee or custodian. While you must begin to receive distributions from the account by the age of seventy and a half, you may provide that your interest will be paid out during the remainder of your life, or the joint life and last survivor expectancy of you and your spouse. If you die before receiving the entire interest in the account, the remaining interest must be distributed to your beneficiaries (or used to purchase an immediate annuity) within five years after your death.

You may set up your account following a Treasury model form. The model trust (Form 5305) and model custodial account agreement (Form 5305A) meet the requirements of an exempt IRA and so do not require a ruling or determination letter approving the exemption of the account and the deductibility of contributions made to the account. If you use this method, you still have to find a bank or other institution or trustee to handle your account or investment. If you manage your own IRA, you may not invest in collectibles. Such an investment is deemed to be a distribution subject to premature withdrawal penalties.

ANNUITY

An annuity, which is purchased through insurance companies, is merely a plan by which you are guaranteed an income for your lifetime. The principal is never exhausted and you need never face the day when your income has dried up. If you have no annuity, but instead have a fixed amount of cash, you may outlive your money. With an annuity the insurance company takes the risk of your longevity. The gamble is the reverse of insurance, where you get the most for dying the earliest. With an annuity you get more by outliving your normal lifespan as measured by the actuarial tables.

Annuities can be joint, first paying to you and then to your spouse for life. You can get them for a specified time so that if you die earlier than expected your beneficiary keeps collecting until the term is over. In choosing annuities compare them as you do life insurance, for cost, service, and fringe benefits. Also check on the withdrawal policy in case you need the lump sum back.

Annuities can be purchased for the first time at retirement. You pay a lump sum and get a monthly income. They can also be deferred, bought early in life and collected at retirement. Your contribution to the annuity is not tax deductible, but the interest that accumulates is not taxed until it is withdrawn.

RETIREMENT BONDS

The Federal Reserve Bank or the Treasury sells retirement bonds which pay interest, compounded semiannually, but cease paying interest when you reach age seventy and a half. If you buy a bond and redeem it within twelve months, no interest is paid and you may not deduct your cost.

IRA INVESTMENTS

Once you have set up an IRA how should you invest your money? At first you will be limited to investments that cost very little ($2,000 in the first year, a bit more than $4,000 in the second year, etc.). You also wish to have taxable investments, since an IRA makes them tax-deferred. Further, you need relative safety and high returns (this is for your retirement, after all). The following is a list of the most favored types of investments for IRAs. The best approach is to invest in fixed-income securities, which are long-term when interest rates are high and short-term when interest rates are low. Set a retirement goal, such as one and a half million dollars. When your pension or other retirement vehicles will eventually meet this goal you can "invest for appreciation" with your IRA, but not before. First, try these high-income investments, as outlined in "A Guide To Investment Selections For Your Merrill Lynch Retirement Plans Account."

U.S. Treasury Bills. Every week the U.S. Treasury issues Treasury Bills to finance the government's short-term debt. Most bills at issuance have a life span of three or six months, and are available in minimum denominations of $10,000. Once a month, the Treasury also offers bills of almost one year's duration.

U.S. Treasury Notes. Once you get to maturities of a year or longer, the next security encountered is a U.S. Treasury Note. Notes run from one to ten years in length and, unlike Treasury Bills, aren't discount issues, but instead make semiannual interest payments. Denominations are usually $5,000 or $10,000, but occasionally notes of small denominations are offered.

U.S. Treasury Bonds. Finally, any U.S. Treasury security of longer than ten years' duration is called a Treasury Bond. As with any other bonds, of course, Treasuries' yields in the open market change along with the yields of other competing bonds. Because the U.S. Government has the largest debt of any organization in the country, and because U.S. Government debt is considered the most secure of any in the world, the interest that the U.S. Government will pay on its securities tends to have the greatest impact of all the many competitors wanting to use your money. The government usually pays the lowest rate of all competitors for your money.

Government Agency Issues. Established over the years by successive Acts of Congress, some agency issues are backed by the full faith and credit of the United States, while others are guaranteed by the issuing agency. Sophisticated buyers know one shining fact about these agency bonds: not one has ever defaulted. Historically, agency issues have offered higher yields than Treasury Bills, Notes, or Bonds; therefore, some people consider this area of the bond market to be particularly attractive.

Quite a few different Government agencies issue bonds. One of them, the Federal Farm Credit Bureau, is concerned with financing America's agricultural industry.

Then there is the Federal Home Loan Bank system, with twelve banks advancing home mortgage credit to some 5,000 savings and loan institutions. The Government National Mortgage Association (GNMA or "Ginnie Mae") also helps provide the credit to satisfy America's need for homes.

GNMAs. "Ginnie Maes" are securities designed to help finance more housing in the United States. They are an offshoot of bonds, so to speak, made up of real estate mortgages. A Ginnie Mae security makes the holder the owner of a share in a pool of Government-guaranteed VA and FHA mortgages. Ginnie Mae holders are guaranteed timely payment of principal and interest by the U.S. Government. Unlike bonds, these securities make monthly distributions. And each check not only includes interest, but also (like a mortgage) returns some of the buyer's invested capital. Ginnie Mae securities come in a minimum denomination of $25,000 and have an average life span of 12 years.

It's also possible to invest in Ginnie Maes through a unit investment trust with around $1,000.

Zero Coupon Bonds. Zero Coupon Bonds, a special group of corporate bonds, may be particularly useful for tax-sheltered retirement accounts. Like the familiar Series E Savings Bonds, you buy Zero Coupons at a substantial discount from par ($250, for example), and you collect par value ($1,000) at maturity. The discount from par is considered ordinary income each year but the taxes are deferred in the IRA, Keogh, and SEP plans, and there is no problem of reinvesting income and virtually no call or refunding risk.*

IRA deductibility depends on 1) how much you earn and 2) whether you are otherwise covered by a pension. Regardless of earnings you get your deduction if you are not covered by any other plan. If you and your spouse earn $50,000 together or you alone earn $35,000 and are covered by any other plan the contribution *is not* deductible. If either of you are covered and you earn between $40,000 and $50,000 together or between $25,000 and $35,000 singly you get only a partial deduction; however, if you jointly earn less than $40,000 or singly earn less than $25,000 you get your full deduction even if otherwise covered. Remember, the tax deferred nature of the IRA remains for everyone.

EMPLOYER PLANS

If your employer has an IRA plan that allows contributions, you can make yours directly to that plan. The rules for IRA contributions to employer-sponsored plans are the same as for personal IRAs, except that distributions from such plans need not start at age seventy and a half. You may make nondeductible contributions to an employer plan and still have an outside IRA. To do this you must immediately designate the contribution as nondeductible. This means you can have a $2,000 IRA *and* contribute a tax-deferred but nondeductible sum to an employer plan.

*Reprinted by permission of Merrill Lynch, Pierce, Fenner & Smith Incorporated. © Copyright 1983 Merrill Lynch, Pierce, Fenner & Smith Incorporated.

IRA FOR GROWTH

Once you have substantially met your goal, or to help push it along, try one of the combined growth and income vehicles. There are a variety available, usually in the form of limited partnership; ask your broker.

SPOUSAL IRA

If you have a spouse who is not working at all and the two of you file a joint return, you can set up an IRA pension fund for your spouse and get a deduction from *your* income tax of $2,250, or an amount equal to your compensation for that taxable year, whichever is less. When you set up the accounts they need not be evenly divided. One can have as little as $250 and the other as much as $2,000. Under the new law, a spouse with some earnings can elect to set up his/her own acount or set aside $250 with you.

Once you have reached the age of seventy and a half you will get no deductions for contributions you make—so make your contributions early. Remember also that you can't use an employer's plan for a spousal contribution.

If at least five years prior to a divorce your ex-spouse had set up an IRA, and for at least three of those years contributed to the account for you, you can continue to make contributions even after the divorce. In this case, the amount you can contribute is the lesser of $1,125 or the sum of your yearly compensation and alimony, support, or maintenance includable in your gross income for income tax purposes.

You can make your contribution anytime within your taxable year and even after, up to your final extension date. So if you get an extension through April 15, which is possible, you could make a contribution to your own pension as late as four months after the usual April 15 filing.

The annual maximum employee contribution under 401K plans would be reduced to $7,000 from the current $30,000. The $7,000 limit would be coordinated with elective deferrals under simplified employee pensions (SEP). The $7,000 cap will be indexed for inflation beginning in 1988. Employers still may make contributions on behalf of the employee up to the current $30,000 limit.

410K PLANS

One might well ask how a self-employed professioal can ever afford to retire. The answer is that we can all have retirement plans, but we must build them ourselves.

If you are self-employed, you can set up a *Keogh plan* and make contributions every year that are deductible from your gross income. Contributions are limited to an amount equal to the lesser of $15,000 or 15 percent of your earned income up to $200,000. If you overfund a Keogh in any given year you can withdraw the surplus before the deadline for filing your income tax return. Like someone with an employer plan, if you have a Keogh you can have an IRA too.

The money can be placed in a bank account, in certificates of deposit, or in an investment program with a brokerage house, which will buy stocks and bonds for your Keogh. The types of purchases that can be made are practically infinite; they include everything from horse farms to stock, and from stock options to real estate—but no collectibles. The important thing is that to avoid being taxed on the income that you make from these contributions, you cannot take any of the money until you are fifty-nine and a half yers old, or become disabled or die. When you retire and pull out your money you will be taxed, but only at your tax rate at that time. If you terminate a Keogh the distribution will not be considered premature.

If you hold shares in a Subchapter "S" corporation (one

with ten or fewer shareholders who have elected to take special tax treatment), you can also create a qualified pension plan. All the Keogh rules regarding amount of contributions and tax savings apply.

The truth is that very little is available to the true independent. Although under the new tax law 25 percent of health insurance costs are deductible. We are no longer pioneers working singly on the frontier. The best that an individual professional can do is an IRA or Keogh-type plan. For more than that, you are simply going to have to get partners. It doesn't matter whether they are for working purposes or planning purposes—you will be much better off if you don't go it alone.

Minimally, if you have an association of several doctors, lawyers, accountants, or the like, which has continuity (it will continue despite the death of one of the parties), centralized management, free transferability (the interest can be transferred to a nonmember without the approval of the others), and limited liability (no one member will be personally responsible for the debts of the association), you will be entitled to develop your own group pension plan and group insurance. If you don't meet these criteria, you will have a problem with the IRS. To clinch the success of your association, simply incorporate. The now-popular professional corporation has been recognized in the majority of states. Those that don't have general recognition do permit such incorporation for practitioners of medicine, dentistry, and law.

A corporation permits you to develop qualified pension plans, profit-sharing plans, and all the life insurance benefits of any corporation. Look back to the retirement devices we've just discussed; you can have those things too. The problem is to have sufficient cash flow to fund them, and that's where an expert professional pension planner comes in. You can contact these experts at banks and pension planning firms, which advertise on the radio and in the newspaper.

A word to those of you who are at the very beginning of the wealth-building years. I suggest that you invest a few hundred dollars in an interview and discussion with professional pension planners, even though you might not have any partners or anyone to join with. This may help you decide how quickly you should associate yourself when it becomes worthwhile to do so. I will tell you this: at some point, it is not only worthwhile but essential to do so in order to develop your retirement program. Don't be a dinosaur; don't practice alone for financial planning.

11

Everybody's
Favorite Service—
The IRS

HERE IS A CRASH, AND I DO MEAN CRASH, COURSE in personal income tax. Those of you who start in ignorance may be better off, since the rules have changed dramatically with the new tax law. You will want to find and use an accountant. Of course, you will continue to read and learn from the many books on the subject. This chapter will simply give you some of the basics, including tips especially appropriate for those in the wealth-building years, and, in general, point you in the right direction.

Incredible as it may seem, income tax was not always inevitable and, in fact, did not exist before 1913. Today we have federal, state, and city taxes to contend with. Since state and city taxes vary depending on where you live, we will concentrate on the federal income tax.

If you are very young and earning little, you may think about preparing your own tax returns for a year or two. I hope you don't. Get used to dealing with professionals; take a look at the section on how to be taken seriously by an accountant (Chapter 12), and start early. The fundamentals of taxation, though, should be grasped by everyone. They are:

- Filing status
- Progressive taxation
- Tax computation
- Tax deduction
- Tax exemption
- Tax credits
- Special benefits (such as capital gains)
- Depreciation, depletion allowance
- Income averaging
- Special problems—recapture, alternative minimum tax
- The IRS itself—filings, audits, and refunds

If you have a passing acquaintance with each of these elements, you will become far more comfortable with our tax system and your own money. We will take a look at them all in this chapter.

There is another element to grasping tax issues as well—that is, preparing you to explore your "tax outlook." How do you see taxes? Some people just pay them; they have no desire to work at saving taxes. Many wealthy people do not take advantage of tax loopholes. Other people pay tax reluctantly and work at saving taxes with a passion. Oddly enough, I had two low-income clients who were heavily audited because they participated in a scheme to take massive tax deductions by incorporating a so-called religious institution. They paid $6,000 to a fraudulent "church" for the privilege of saving taxes even though they were in low brackets. Why do otherwise honest, hard-working people get into so much trouble with the IRS? Perhaps the government seems so impersonal that morality is no longer an issue. Perhaps the inability to budget is so ingrained that they cannot pay the tax. But probably it is because of a complete ignorance of legitimate ways to avoid, not evade, taxes.

I get annoyed at the timid taxpayer. Yes, the IRS can audit you and can even impose penalties. But most often they allow deductions, settle, eliminate penalties, and agree to payouts. I have known people to pay far too much because they were scared of taking legitimate deductions or were overly wary of tax-sheltered investments. Don't be this way yourself. Choose your investments to minimize or reduce taxes wherever possible. In Chapters 2 and 10 you learned the power of tax-free growth. Every tax-saving opportunity brings you close to economic freedom. If you were very disciplined, you would invest your tax savings and be amazed at the wealth you would accumulate.

FILING STATUS

The amount of tax you will actually pay is a function of your tax status and your total taxable income in any given year. In turn, your tax status is a function of who you are in life and your total taxable income is a function of how much you have earned, deducted, and invested. This will determine your tax bracket. Status and bracket are two often-overlooked facts of a tax life.

As far as tax status goes, there are the following possibilities. If you are married, you are usually best off filing as a married couple filing jointly. To do this you must be legally married on the last day of the year for which you are filing. You do not have to be living together as long as you remain legally married. However, if you are legally separated, under a final decree of divorce or final decree of separation, you cannot file jointly. If you just have a separation agreement, you can still file jointly. For some types of deductions, you *must* file jointly—for example, if you have a contribution to make to an IRA for a nonworking spouse. On joint returns, each spouse is liable for the entire tax and if one does not pay the other must. They may however not be criminally responsible for fraud unless they actively participated.

If you are married there are some circumstances under which you cannot file jointly. For young people it is important to know that if either you or your spouse is supported as a dependent by someone else, such as a parent, you cannot file jointly. If your spouse decides because you had a tiff to sign a separate return you cannot force him or her to file jointly. If you have different recording years (highly unlikely), you cannot file jointly.

If you and your spouse have split and you do not want to file jointly, you can qualify to file as an unmarried and use the single person rate. If you maintain a separate household with the children you can claim the child as a dependent and file as single head of household. If you provide over half the cost of the supporting household even though your child does not live with you, you can use head-of-household rates provided you meet the usual tests for head of household, which are: you and your spouse cannot be married at the end of the year; you maintain a household for an entire year for a dependent relative; the household is your main residence; you pay more than one half the cost to maintain the household; you are a citizen or a U.S. alien resident. If you are not a head of household and you are not married, you file at a single-person rate. However, if the reason you are unmarried is that you are a widow or widower you can use special surviving spouse rates, which are the same as if you filed a joint return. But this is only for the year in which your spouse died; after that, you must file singly.

The most important thing about selecting these statuses is that you are subject to different tax tables. The following are the statuses in descending order of amount of taxation. Next to each status is the tax you would pay, all things being equal, on earnings of $20,000.

PROGRESSIVE TAXATION AND THE TAX TABLES

Once you have determined your tax status, you now have to determine how much tax you will pay.

Even under the new law we are subject to a progressive

although simplified progressive tax system. This means, as your income rises your bracket does as well. It is important to watch out for your marginal income. Many times people are asked, "What is your marginal tax?" and they have no idea. Marginal tax merely means the last tax bracket you were in for the last amount you earned. For example, your first $20,000 may be taxed at only 15 percent, but if you earn $90,000 your last $10,000 might be taxed at 33 per cent.

Under prior law, income was taxed under a 14-bracket system of rates ranging from 11 percent to 50 percent. The simplified new tax bill provides for only two brackets, with rates of 15 and 28 percent. The 28-percent rate applies to taxable income levels of $29,750 for married couples filing jointly, $17,850 for single filers, and $25,290 for heads of household.

In addition, a 5% surcharge is levied against upper-income level taxpayers in order to eliminate the benefit to them of the 15-percent rate and the personal exemption. This surcharge will create an effective top marginal rate of 33 percent.

The change to the tax rate structure will be phased in during 1987, so you will have a five-bracket system for that year. The top 1987 bracket for married couples will be 38.5% for income in excess of $90,000. For incomes of $45,000 to $90,000, the rate will be 35%. For incomes of $28,000 to $45,000, the rate will be 28%. For incomes of $3,000 to $28,000, the rate will be 15%, and for income under $3,000 the rate will be 11%. In addition, the 5 percent surcharge against the high-income individuals will not begin until 1988.

TAX COMPUTATION

Your basic tax will be determined by taking all your items included in gross income, adjusting them by deducting certain adjustments from gross income, to arrive at your *adjusted gross income*. After determining this, you take certain deductions. It is these deductions that most new taxpayers concentrate on.

However, they are the simplest elements to know and understand. Your average tax preparer probably knows them by heart. After you've taken your deductions from adjusted gross income, you arrive at your *taxable income*. From that you take certain exemptions. When you've arrived at your exemptions, you've arrived at your tax. But that's not the end. You then look at the tax table to see how much tax you would pay. You still don't have your final answer, however, because from your final tax you deduct again a category of items called *tax credits*.

These are coveted dollar-for-dollar deductions from the actual tax—not from your gross income, not from your adjusted gross income, but from your tax itself. When you have made that deduction you know how much you should pay, and then you pay it.

A run-down of these items would take a book in itself. However, here's a quick idea so that you get the gist of what taxation is all about.

Gross Income

Gross income really means all the types of income on which the government wants to collect taxes. It is here that the government gives its incentives and disincentives. The kinds of earnings that it wishes to encourage in the American people it taxes less, and perhaps does not even include in gross income. Some items of gross income are your salaries, wages, bonuses and commmissions, and your professional fees. If you are an entrepreneur or had your own business, you have to file a Schedule C, which lists everything you earned from your own business. You would also have to file a Schedule SE, which is a self-employed tax that is paid largely to Social Security for your benefit in the future. Not only earnings from labor go into gross income—rents, royalties, dividends from stocks, alimony that's being paid to you, even gambling and lottery winnings are included as well. If your employer contributed to an employment plan, you must check whether some of these contributions are also included. Under special complicated rules foreign earned income is included, as is the income from selling your residence. There are some exemptions to the latter; for example, should you buy a new primary residence within two years no money need be included in gross income. If you are over fifty-five and did not want to buy a new residence you can exclude $125,000 of any gain.

In short, most of the kinds of money that you expect to make are considered gross income and would be included. Some things, however, are not included. Should you be fortunate enough to get a gift or an inheritance, none of that would be included. Social Security benefits, scholarships meeting certain rules, educational assistance and aid, and many types of fringe benefits and medical benefits paid by an employer are not included. Alimony and child support payments are not included. Interestingly, if you collect in a personal injury matter that too is excluded from gross income, as are your disability payments should you buy disability insurance and then not be able to work. Before the new law up to $200.00 of dividend income for married couples and $100.00 for single taxpayers was exempt. Starting in 1987 this is no longer the case.

Income Averaging

Income averaging has been eliminated for tax years on and after 1987.

Capital Gains

The new law repeals the net capital gain deduction for individuals. Capital gains will be taxed at regular rates, up to 28 percent. If the taxpayer incurs capital gains while subjet to the 5 percent surcharge, the marginal tax rate on those gains is effecting 33%. The maximum 28 percent rate will apply in 1987 even though some individuals will pay higher tax at higher rates under the blended five-bracket system for that year.

Losses from the sale or exchange of capital assets are deductible to the extent of gains from the sale or exchange of capital assets, plus $3,000. All net capital losses will be deductible on a dollar-for-dollar basis against ordinary income, subject to the annual $3,000 limit. Excess losses will carry over to subsequent years in the same manner as is provided under current law.

A capital gains tax is an incentive, not a special annoyance. It is a tax imposed on profits made from the investment of money (capital). The government encourages investment of capital in things—it would rather you spend your money investing in oil wells than buying personal luxuries. Therefore, Uncle Sam gives you a break on profits from investments. Let's see how this works.

There are two kinds of capital gains, a long-term and a short-term. If you own an asset for one year or less and then sell it, this is short-term. If ownership is for over a year, it is long-term. It is the long-term gains that get the special income tax treatment; a short-term gain does not. This is why people hold assets for at least a year. Under the terms of the special treatment, the tax rate is the same as for your ordinary income, but the capital gains tax is imposed on only 40 percent of the profit you receive. Sixty percent of the profit is subtracted from your gross income before the gain is taxed.

Capital gains tax is figured not on the gross profit or gain, but on the net profit or gain, called "basis." To figure out the basis, take the sale price and deduct the "adjusted basis," which is your original purchase price plus additional money you spent on capital improvements. This gives us the formula:

Basis = sale price minus adjusted basis (original purchase price + capital expenditures)

For example, if land is sold at a profit, you have captial gains tax to pay, not ordinary income tax. If you bought the land for $25,000 and you sell it for $35,000 after putting in a $1,000 septic tank, you have an adjusted basis of $26,000. Your net profit or basis is then $9,000. It is on this amount that the tax is imposed. If you had bad luck and the selling price was less than the adjusted basis, you have a capital loss.

You may have heard that since E.R.T.A., capital gains tax has been reduced to a maximum of 20 percent; the old maximum was 28 percent. How is this calculated? Under E.R.T.A. the maximum tax rate is 50 percent on any type of income. However, a profit from the investment of capital is not taxed entirely; only 40 percent of the profit is taxed at the maximum rate of 50 percent. Fifty percent of 40 percent is 20 percent; therefore, if you do have a gain from the investment of capital, the tax you pay is a maximum of 20 percent of the net profit. If you are not in the top 50 percent bracket, your "maximum tax" will be even less, that is, 40 percent of profit multiplied by the amount in your tax bracket equals capital gains tax. By the way, this 20 percent maximum tax applies to profits made June 9, 1981, or thereafter.

A good thing to do with certain property is to take depreciations. Since you haven't actually sold the property, there is no real loss. Yet Uncle Sam lets you deduct about a fifth of the value of the property from your tax each year. If you then sell the property at a gain, all this depreciation has to be subtracted from the original purchase price to reach the adjusted basis.

Those of you 55 or older, or with a spouse 55 or older, can save a whopping capital gains tax when you sell your home. You may exclude up to $125,000 of the profit, provided it is your primary residence (house, co-op, or condominium) and you owned and occupied it for at least three of the five preceding year. This exemption applies to residences sold July 20, 1981, or thereafter. For anybody else, the gain is not taxed if you reinvest the proceeds in another primary residence within twenty-four months after you make the sale. More than one sale and purchase are permitted if the relocation takes place because of employment.

What if you have capital losses? With short-term losses (property held for one year or less), you get a dollar-for-dollar deduction from gross income. For long-term losses (property held for one year or more) you can use only up to 50 percent to offset ordinary income, and then up to a $3,000 maximum.

Any loss over this amount can be carried forward to the next year. Uncle Sam isn't giving anything away. You can't create losses with sales between husbands and wives. Nor can you take a loss if you have a wash sale—that is, a sale of securities at a loss made thirty days before or after the purchase of identical securities. For example, if you owned $10,000 worth of stock and needed the money quickly, you could sell it at $34 instead of your purchase price of $35. However, if two weeks later you rebought the stock in exactly the same amounts you could not take a loss.

Deductions

After arriving at gross income, you may then deduct certain limited items to arrive at *adjusted gross income*. These so-called adjustments to income fall into two basic categories: the cost of earning your gross income, and the money you have been able to "sock away" for your retirement. In the former case, the cost of doing business is reflected for entrepreneurs on Schedule C before they arrive at the true income they receive from their business. For salaried people, deductions regarding unreimbursed travel expenses, clothing, and other adjustments can be made at this point in the tax return. Again, it's essential to have a tax preparer who knows your business and knows what's allowed to be deducted. For example, I have clients who are photographers and stylists. That means they spend their life shopping for things that help set up a photograph, such as the beautiful fruit you might see on the cover of a cooking magazine. Some of these things they use themselves, others of them are strictly business. It becomes essential to keep detailed records. Here is where an audit, if any, can go smoothly if you know what you spent and to what purpose.

Of greater importance to your investment strategy is the fact that your IRA and Keogh payments can be deducted from your gross income to arrive at adjusted gross income. This is what I meant in Chapter 10 when I wrote that the IRAs and

Keoghs give you a double deduction, something that no other investment can give. That is, not only do your earnings accumulate tax-deferred, but the amount you put away is itself deducted, and you never pay income tax on that original earned amount until it grows and is withdrawn in the normal course of your retirement.

After you have arrived at adjusted gross income, you take your *deductions*. As I previously mentioned, this is the place where most taxpayers get hung up, yet it's the easiest to understand. Deductions from adjusted gross income may be itemized or standard. There is a $1,000 standard deduction for those of you who do not feel you have enough deductions to exceed $1,000. You will take a flat sum and be done with it. Those who feel they can itemize deductions should remember a few of these: the first $100 on dividend income (or $200 for a joint return) can be deducted; certain tax for income on local and government bonds can be deducted; bad debts and business losses are important deductions. Without becoming overly sophisticated, there is a special filing that a corporation may do called a Subchapter "S" filing. These so-called Subchapter "S" corporations, if they suffer a loss, can permit each individual shareholder to take that loss from their own adjusted gross income rather than having the corporation take the loss. Many people invest in corporations that can become a Subchapter "S." In this way, even if the enterprise fails, they will get a deduction even though they may not get a profit.

If you use your home or automobile as a business expense, or have invested in real estate and received depreciation deductions, these are all deducted here. Once again, it becomes clear that the government wants you to invest your capital in something that will build the country. As the government makes decisions as to where best use of private funds can be made, tax breaks evolve. Depreciation deductions for real estate (discussed below), deductions for interest that you paid on loans, capital losses, and oil and gas depletion allowances all come into play here.

A special type of deduction called a *depreciation deduction* is available to those who own real estate in which they do not reside. The concept is that a building deteriorates or depreciates in value as it becomes older. This is not always the case in reality, though—the value of a building in a highly growing area may actually rise as years go by. Nevertheless, it cannot be disputed that buildings do have life cycles. Under the law a building is considered to have deteriorated or depreciated in value to zero in a period of 18 years. This means that theoretically a taxpayer could deduct 1/18 of the value of a building every year for the first 18 years of ownership. After the eighteenth year there would be no depreciation deduction, since the building would be deemed to have "fully depreciated." Such deduction is called a "straight line depreciation." Depreciation can also be accelerated, however. Many people wish to do this because they do not intend to own a building for an eighteen-year period of time. To accelerate depreciation, one can take the full depreciation over a period of only five years. This gives very heavy tax deductions in the first five years of ownership of the building. However, if the building is sold before the eighteen-year period has elapsed, the extra deductions that were taken are charged back to the taxpayer—a practice called *recapture of depreciation.*

Any depreciation plan must be discussed carefully with your accountant. But whatever you choose, you can see that this special deduction is very favorable to the real estate owner. If you buy a limited partnership, a tax shelter, or another type of investment that gives you deductions through depreciation, make sure that you know whether or not there will be a recapture of depreciation somewhere along the line. If you are not prepared for this you may be charged a good deal of tax in a year in which you didn't expect to pay.

Exemptions

Once you have arrived at your taxable income by taking your deductions from adjusted gross income, you can now think about your *exemptions*. If you have children you will receive a $1,000 exemption for every dependent. But children are not the only dependents. You are your own dependent, as is a spouse, as can be your parents. So you have a series of exemptions that you may take from taxable income to arrive at the amount you must use when you hit the tax tables. Of significant importance to young people is whether they themselves are dependents of their parents. If your parents contribute more than one half of your support, you may be their dependent. If they take you as a dependent, you cannot duplicate that. At times, certain financial aid or college scholarships, under very limited circumstances, can also be considered income to you that spoils the dependency exemption your parents might enjoy.

For the older reader, you, your children, perhaps your parents, and your spouse will surely be dependents. Here again is where cash flow and tax savings interact. For example, let us say that you have taken a large loan in order to buy a piece of real estate. You will get a great many deductions for depreciation and interest expenses. You may however be worried that you can't afford to pay back the loan itself. What do you do? You pretend mathematically that these deductions are exemptions, and you translate the value of the deduction into a number of exemptions. For example, if you have $2,000 worth of interest deductions and you are in the 50 percent bracket, consider the exemption to equal 1 ($1,000 = 50% of $2,000). Then go to your employer and increase the amount of exemptions that you told him you would be taking. So if you have one child, one spouse, and yourself, ask for four deductions instead of three. The result will be that your actual weekly paycheck will be higher. Use the extra amount that is not withheld for income tax to pay the loan. In this way you have created a little extra cash flow for yourself during the year instead of having to wait for a tax refund toward the end of the year. Don't overdo this, though; many people, in order to pad their paycheck, take large numbers of exemptions (nine or ten). They get a large paycheck, but very little has been withheld as tax. At the end of the year they are stuck and must pay a good deal of money in taxes. Unless they have been careful to make sure that their tax savings expected from deductions roughly equals the amount of withholding that they are having paid over to themselves, they had better have a good source of funds to pay their taxes at the end of the year.

Once you have taken your exemptions, you then go to the tax table. Look up the tax percentage that applies to the eventual income you've arrived at; that's your tax. Or almost . . .

Tax Credits

There's also such a thing as a *tax credit*. As I mentioned, this is a dollar-for-dollar deduction from your tax, and they are coveted because they are more than deductions—they are total tax savings. There are very few tax credits. Older people receive them just for reaching age sixty-five; the blind and disabled also get them. Other tax credits include: 20% of the cost incurred in rehabilitating historic structures, and 10% incurred on other qualifying buildings such as housing for the elderly. Credits are available too for certain low-income taxpayers who have a child living with them. The maximum credit is $851.

A childcare credit of between $720 and $1440 is available based on the number of children, the cost of care, and the income of the parents. Special credits are also available for those paying taxes to foreign governments.

TAXES AND YOUR INVESTMENT PLANNING

Any good preparer of income tax will know all the types of income included in gross income, the types of items to apply to arrive at adjusted gross income, all the deductions and whether you are entitled to them, the exemptions appropriate to you and your family, and of course the credits that you can take advantage of. It is not in this area that CPAs and accountants get accolades for their sharp tax planning. It is in certain other, more sophisticated, areas that they are involved with and which you should be aware of.

Since you are wealth building, I will concentrate on some of the more important aspects of taxes as they involve investment planning. Here are the concepts that you should grasp for lifelong enjoyment of tax savings:

Taxable vs. Tax-free Income

The income from certain investments—most notably, muncipal bonds—is not included in your gross income. Go back to the chapter on the chemistry of investment and you will see that this feature of tax-free income is the most significant feature of municipal bonds. Now you know that this simply means that any income distributed by the municipality to you as interest from these bonds is not included in your gross income in the first place. Therefore, it never is included in your eventual taxable income and never results in pushing up your tax bracket.

Government bonds (U.S.) are taxable with respect to their income. The state and city do not, however, tax government income. It is possible that under our new tax law state and city taxes will no longer be a deduction on our federal income tax return. If so, government bonds will become more attractive. This is so because we often did not care if we had to pay city or state taxes, since we would deduct them and at least get a deduction from adjusted gross income on our federal return for the money we paid to the state or municipality. If these deductions are no longer available, then we will be very interested in not paying any city or state tax since we will have no side benefit. We can fulfill that by buying U.S. government bonds, paying federal tax but not city or state tax. Most other income is included in gross income. For example, rents from real estate are includable, and dividends from stocks, except for an exclusion of $100 per person per year or $200 per couple per year, are includable. Should you lend money to someone, for a second mortgage, for example, and receive interest from them, this is fully taxable. Should you invest in a mutual fund that pays income, you once again must include this in gross income.

On the other hand, your growth investments will grow every year without paying you income and without being taxed during the year of growth. For example, if you invest in a mutual fund for growth alone that paid no income, there would of course be no income to include for tax purposes. Similarly, if you owned real estate that had appreciated but paid no rent, there would be no tax while you held this asset. These are called purely growth assets and produce no income for you. In your wealth-building years, particularly in the middle of those years, you should be holding largely growth assets. At the very beginning, your income from wages or self-employment might be so low that you need an extra boost from income producing assets. By age thirty-five you might again, perhaps with a family and tuition needs, need some extra income from your investments. However, for true wealth building during the middle period, say twenty-five to thirty or thirty-two, keep those growth assets in mind. While they are growing you will pay no tax. What happens when you sell your growth assets? This brings up a second most important concept regarding taxes and investments.

Bond Swapping

There are several devices that careful investors use to save themselves taxes; bond swapping is one of these. If you do own bonds that have decreased in value, one of the things you should do before the calendar year is out is to sell the bond at a loss. Use the money to buy new bonds that pay the same amount of income. You'll be able to buy the same face value of bonds and receive the same income as long as the maturity date is longer than the bond you sold. Bonds are priced according to many factors—among them the security of the issuer and its credit-worthiness, the amount of interest income paid on the bond, and the maturity date. The longer the maturity date, the cheaper the bond usually is. In order to buy an equivalent bond with respect to rating or credit-worthiness and income, you have to give up something. Give up maturity. You'll preserve the same income that you are used to and have an equally safe bond, but the bond will not mature for a few extra years. Meanwhile, you will have created an income tax deduction by taking the loss on the bond that you did sell. This is bond swapping.

Alternative Minimum Tax

The government believes that it is the job of all Americans to do their best to pay their taxes but not to overpay. However, there is a limit to how much they'll let you get away with. The alternative minimum tax, known as the AMT, is figured out after you have determined your normal tax. The calculation requires the same amount of concentration of income inclusions. However, many deductions and credits are disallowed under the AMT. The AMT is designed so that when you take into consideration your exclusions of dividends, the deductions for oil depletion, accelerated real estate depreciation, and other items known as tax preference items, you cannot reduce your tax below 20 percent. If your ordinary tax has been reduced below the amount of the AMT, then the AMT will apply to you. Tax preference items include the above plus capital gains deductions, incentive stock options, accelerated amortization, intangible drilling costs, and a few others.

The important thing to remember, since you will be using a professional to help you with your AMT calculation, is that it will be incurred if you have an excessive amount of capital gain or other of these tax preference items. Therefore, if you buy a tax shelter in order to save taxes make sure to inquire whether or not there are tax preference items being used to achieve a write-off. In our office we do our best never to suggest that a tax shelter with a tax preference item be purchased. This is so because if tax preferences are too great the client will have to pay the AMT. Basically this means they have overbought their shelter needs, which is never a good idea.

Buying Tax Shelters

One of the best things that the financial planning industry has done for the average investor is to create a professional who has nothing to sell but who can assess tax shelters. No one can tell you whether a tax shelter will actually pay off—make a profit and get you your money back. But there are many indications that when weighed help make the decision of whether to buy in the first place, and which one to buy. Once again a separate book could and should be written for the average consumer on appropriate tax shelters. For now I'm sorry to limit our discussion to just a few brief words with an important caveat. Do get an adviser before you buy a shelter. Tax shelter costs range from between $50,000 to $300,000 for private placements. It is in these areas that you must be most careful. You basically will be signing a note, even though you may put down very little cash, that will obligate you to pay a bank this sum of money over a period of from five to eight years. During this period you are buying the right to take several deductions, usually from adjusted gross income, to arrive at taxable income. Since a young person might be buying a house or be about to incur other large purchases, tax shelters should be the last on your list of priorities. However, if you do have very high income, it is far better to take a calculated risk and give your money to the general partners for a possible investment than to give it away forever to Uncle Sam.

If I could list in order of importance facts to look at in buying a tax shelter, I would say the following:

1. Are you at risk? By this I mean if something should go wrong with the shelter, can you be tapped for any more money than you already pledged when you made the investment? If the answer is yes, do not go into the shelter under any circumstances even if you have the chance to make a fortune. This is sheer madness. You must have enough control over your money to know when and if payments will be required of you.

2. Who are the promoters and the general partners? Tax shelters are so complicated and come with such a large prospectus that most investors forget that the most important thing is still people. How many years have they been in business? How much will they be receiving for selling and for managing the property, etc.?

3. What is the underlying investment all about? If it's real estate, is it the kind of real estate you would want to own if you were rich enough to own the whole piece? Is it a scheme—for example, buying scotch futures from Scotland or irrigating methods for the desert (two shelters that actually did exist)?

4. What do you get? Are you a limited partner? A shareholder in a corporation? Do you have any liability outside your initial investment? Do you understand the invest-

ment? By this I don't mean do you understand the tax implications or legal implications. Do you understand the investment itself? For example, many tax shelters are in research and development of medical equipment. I suggest this type of investment to doctors but not to lawyers. The doctor can assess what he or she thinks of the equipment, and when it will become obsolete. In fact in our office we often call upon our own clients who are in equipment leasing, medicine, or entertainment to take a look at the soundness of the business part of the shelter.

5. Are there tax preference items that might be disallowed if the AMT applies to you?

6. Are there heavy deductions that might be questioned in an IRS audit? For example, is there too much depreciation being taken, are profits being distributed to general partners and being called losses? It's in this area that you need your adviser.

Despite all of these risks, tax shelters remain popular. Even under the possibility that a new law will eliminate most tax shelter savings, general partners are merely rearranging their deals, not going out of business. When a tax shelter works it can be a beautiful thing for us individually and even for the nation. It means that something new has been created—new real estate, new housing, new energy, new medical equipment, new research and development in any phase or area of our industries. It means that the individual investor has been able to get together with other investors and enjoy significant tax deductions sanctioned and approved of by Uncle Sam. It means that after years of enjoying these deductions and making the most of their hard-earned money because taxes have been saved, they will in turn receive more profit from the success of the venture. At its best, it can be great capitalism; at its worst, it can be swindling.

Second Homes Can Result in Tax Savings

We've already discussed some savings received when you sell your primary residence. However, many of you would like a second home. Some of you cannot now afford to buy the first home of your dreams. Yet you find that very nice little house in the country that would work as a second home while you continue to rent your apartment in the city. Whether you can afford it or not depends a great deal on your Pay Yourself First Budget, your concept of leveraging, and whether your parents can help you out. But did you know that you could also take tax deductions for your second home? For example, if you rent a vacation home for less than fifteen days, you cannot deduct any expenses attributed to the rental and if you got a profit on the rental you are not taxed on the profit either. But, if you rent your home for fifteen days or more you can then determine if the personal home meets the fourteen-day or ten-percent test: Whether you personally use your vacation or second home during the year for the greater of fourteen days or ten percent of the number of days the home is rented to someone else, or if you rent your home for more than fifteen days but you don't use it for personal use, you can deduct the expenses in excess of the rental income. If so, you can deduct expenses for renting up to your gross rental income. This means you may be receiving rental income without paying taxes on it.

There are rules for figuring out whether or not you are personally using your home. If you or another person in your immediate family or co-owner use it, it's personal use. In short, if you do own a rental home, and you rent it out for more than fifteen days during the year and you yourself use it for a period exceeding the fifteen (which you probably will), you can still deduct any costs from the income you receive for those fifteen days. Should you rent your second home for a good deal of time during the year and use it only for a small period of time yourself (for example, you own a ski house, renting it out for skiers and coming there only during the summer), then you can even take deductions that far exceed the rental income that you receive.

If You Own Stock

Remember, of course, to work through the capital gains structure. Buy or sell in the proper years. By this I mean if you have a long-term gain that you want to take, try to realize a long-term loss in the same year. Match up your short-term gains against your short-term losses. If you have no losses perhaps you would like to defer the gain and sell next year. In addition, if you buy a mutual fund, ask the salesman or your adviser whether that fund has accumulated capital gains during the year. If so, they may pay that out to you and you will have an unexpected capital gains tax to pay on money that you really didn't want distributed to you at all. If you do sell the mutual fund then there is an average cost of sale method that is applied to determine whether you have capital gains or not. Obviously, since mutual funds deal with hundreds of issues of stock, the record keeping is almost impossible if you would have to find out exactly which stocks you own, when and which were sold when you sold your shares in the mutual fund itself. There are two methods of calculating your tax, the single-category and the double-category methods. In either case your tax preparer should understand and apply the method. You should at least know the names so you can be sure that you ask whether the methods were being used and which one best suited your needs. If you own stocks with big dividends, don't forget your exclusion of $100 or $200 on a joint return. Buying stock that sells with tax-free dividends or stock dividends is another way of avoiding income tax on dividend income.

To compare interest rates on taxable funds with those on nontaxable funds, do the following calculation: subtract your tax bracket from 100 percent and multiply that figure by the interest on the taxable fund. If a taxable mutual fund offered 13.5 percent and a tax-free bond offered 9 percent, which one should you buy? If you were in the 30 percent bracket, your formula would be:

$$100\% - 30\% = 70\% \times 13.5\% = .0945 \ (9.45\%)$$

The taxable fund would therefore be better than the tax-free bond.

Although it is complicated beyond the experience of even many real estate attorneys, a tax-free real estate exchange is possible. If you do hold property for business purposes and are fortunate enough to find another piece of property of equal type and value, you can exchange it without paying a capital gains tax. These tax-free exchanges are very difficult to achieve since finding the perfect property is like finding the perfect mate. However, I was able to effect such an exchange of hotels twice during my career. With so much real estate for sale and so much need for innovation in the field, it is actually becoming easier to make exchanges. But remember, this must be business property or a property held for commercial purposes or resell purposes. For example, you cannot swap your condominium in New York for a condominium in San Maarten. However, if you held your condominium in New York for rental purposes or business purposes, or plan to develop it in some way, you could swap it for the same property value in San Maarten if it too was held for business purposes. The basis and other capital gain consequences to you when you finally do sell must be considered when you make your tax-free swap.

Tax-free exchanges really start getting complex when you go into multiparty deals. You may find a piece of property owned by individual B. Individual C wants to buy your property. You make arrangements whereby C acquires property B and then you exchange your property A for B. If these alphabet letters are getting on your nerves, think of what it's like at the closing. A lawyer once remarked to me that he was thinking of getting a dining room table instead of a conference table for his office, so that when he had tax-free exchanges he could put an extra leaf in and expand his seating area.

Using Your Family

In my book *Your Kids, Your Money,* I devote many chapters to saving taxes by transferring property to your children, hiring them, and making intrafamily loans. The essence of all of these suggestions is transferring income and ownership to another family member in a lower income bracket. By all means read the book, and at the very least remember that these options are available to you and should be discussed with an adviser.

DEALING WITH THE IRS

With all these fun and games, why is it then that people get into so much trouble trying to evade taxes? There are no penalties, only rewards, for avoiding taxes. *Evading* taxes—taking deductions that don't exist, deliberately failing to report income—is just plain stupid. These two sins I've just mentioned are very different, however. The willful refusal to declare income is hiding your money from the federal government, pure and simple. It is a crime and subject to civil penalties. Taking deductions that may be in error results in an audit and maybe some payment at worst with a penalty, usually a waived penalty, to the government.

The style you should take is honest aggressiveness. Most people develop a tax style and suffer with it all their lives. There's the person who doesn't start doing his income tax returns until April 12 and is the last one to get to the mailbox at midnight on April 15. There's the worrier who thinks about it all year long and is so scared of taxes that he never makes an investment because he might be taxed on the profit. There's the abdicator who gives over the whole thing to a spouse or accountant and doesn't want to know about it. We usually hear these people say, "I don't know anything about numbers."

There's the human calculator who figures and figures until he and everyone in his family is blue in the face, so that they get the last penny out of their investment. Had they spent their time enjoying a long cool drink, going to a museum, or even working for extra income, they might have been better off.

What does the IRS really do with your tax return? First they look for math errors and do checks on the following types of "funny stuff"—dividend exclusion in excess of $100 per person or $200 on a joint return; incorrectly reported income as checked against the W-2 and 1099 form you gave them; fractional exemptions, which are not allowed; casualty and theft losses and medical expenses that don't match up to the amount of adjusted gross income you must have to take such deductions; how you've used your auto mileage; whether your household child-care deductions match up with the income you must have in order to get such deductions. These are basically mechnical, mathematical corrections they may make and they'll let you know about them by mail. It often takes up to two years for them to get around to you so don't hold your breath and don't worry. But the computer may single you out for a more thorough examination. If so it will take place in a dreadfully dreary IRS office. Bring all the documentation you can find or, better yet, send an adviser and stay home yourself. Many people who are very good at record keeping even enjoy an audit. I have two such clients.

One *can* win with the IRS, because they are making an inquiry, not conducting a witch hunt. If you can't document or they disagree with you, you make a deal. Deals can be made for the amount of money that should be paid and even for the pay-out term. If no settlement is reached, you'll get a ninety-day letter, also called a "notice of deficiency." That means they will impose an additional tax. If you still disagree with them, then you go to tax court. Alternatively you can pay the tax, ask for a refund claim, and then go to the Federal District Court or the U.S. Court of Claims. Here's where you need a tax lawyer.

The tax court does have a small tax case procedure for deficiencies under $5,000. I know several people who have filed cases on their own and won. Anything above that I suggest you do get help.

There is also a Taxpayer Compliance Measurement Program (TCMP) audit. This is what everyone hates because it seems unfair. It's a random audit selected by computer just to see if everything's going okay, like a spot check at the border. You may have to go through an audit just because the computer picked you. Naturally, there is a statute of limitation—three years—on all of this. But if you fail to report an item of gross income or more than 25 percent of the gross income reported there is six-years statute of limitation. Interest is also charged on the deficiencies.

But there is such a thing as a Taxpayer Bill of Rights. Your rights are implemented in a variety of ways, including:

- Privacy and confidentiality, with the right to have your personal and financial information kept confidential and to know why information is requested.
- Courtesy and consideration from all IRS personnel.
- Payment of only the required tax: You have the right to plan so that you pay the *least* tax due under the law.
- Fairness if your return is examined, including convenient scheduling and the right of representation.
- The right to appeal.
- A fair collection process, including a notice or a bill for unpaid tax in clear and understandable language.
- Answers to your telephone tax questions.
- You have the right to get special help from the taxpayer ombudsman if you have a tax problem you cannot resolve through normal channels.

All in all, as I've noted, it's a good idea to use an accountant for preparation of the tax return. But how do you find one? What do they charge? Can you get accountants (and other financial professionals) to take you seriously? These and other related questions are dealt with in the next chapter.

12

How to Get Professionals to Take You Seriously

Y OU MAY NEED A LAWYER, you must have an accountant, and you probably want a broker. But they may not want you. Since you are young and just starting out, professionals may feel that you cost them more money than you're worth. You need a lot of help and a lot of their time, and they can obtain precious little in fees or commissions from you. Yet you are a consumer and you are entitled to be treated with respect and to be treated fairly. How do you make that delicate marriage between the right professional and yourself? You'll find that the successful money managers are those who rely at least to some extent on the advice of others. The more successful an individual is, the more you will find a mentor or adviser in the background.

To be a respected client of a respectable professional you need to do a few minor things that will make all the difference in the world. First, you must remember that professionals have only their time to sell. If you forget that you will overuse the time of a professional to no avail. Basically you will become a pest. This is okay, but only if you pay for it, and even then a professional with self-respect will shun even the richest, most mature client who does nothing but waste his brain power on minor issues.

Apart from respecting the time value of professional practice, a second rule is to present yourself to professionals in a way that indicates that you will be a good future prospect. In other words, you try to look like a client who will be meaningful to them some day. You do this in the same way as you would approach someone for a loan or a job. You put your best foot forward and convince the professionals that they should do work for you at lower, moderate, sometimes even *ridiculous* fees because you will be loyal to them when you really make it in the future.

A third thing never to be forgotten is that professionals were also young once and may actually remember when that was the case. Some professionals like occasionally to be educators for receptive young people. They like somebody who respects them and is enthusiastic. They also like to see worlds other than their own dull four-cornered office, no matter how picturesque the view or posh the leather on the chairs. If you can bring with you the freshness of a field that you are enthusiastic about (are you an artist or actor, do you have plans for a new business that captures the imagination?) you will have a professional friend for life.

In return you will get a good deal more than help and more advice than you would ever have expected, and more than you could ever afford to pay for. Speaking of paying, always find out precisely what you are going to be charged. Some professionals may seem friendly and helpful and may even lure you into believing they're not going to charge you, or perhaps charge you very little. Then you get a whopping bill. Blame yourself, because you must always ask what the costs will be.

By and large all the money professionals—your attorney, accountant, broker, insurance agent, and financial planner—are cut from relatively the same cloth. They should have solid educational credentials and fifteen or so years in their business, and they should be keeping abreast of new trends in their fields. It is a mistake for you to go with a professional as young as you; they cannot teach you enough. Let them find their own way. You need someone who can really take you by the hand—the higher-paid, more established professional. On the other hand, you don't want the major law firm, the Big Eight accounting firm, or the huge, impersonal brokerage house. You are simply not big enough for them and you will get lost in the shuffle. Ultimately if they accept you as a client, you will become an experimental case for one of their younger people.

LAWYERS AND ACCOUNTANTS

While there are differences among professions, certain guidelines apply to lawyers and accountants alike. The following is an adaptation of an article entitled "Calling in the Law: What to Do When It's Time to Talk to an Attorney," which I wrote with Judy R. Block for *Working Woman* magazine. While the article is now over five years old, the response has been fantastic, and the rules of the game haven't changed. It has now been adapted to apply to accountants as well.

Organize Your Thoughts Before You See a Professional

Have a clear idea of what you want to say before your initial meeting. You'll waste a lot of valuable time if you leave out any of the details of your case. And remember, incorrect or misleading information can have serious consequences.

Ask for a Consultation

A consultation—a preliminary session with a professional you have not yet hired—has several purposes. It gives you the opportunity to state the facts of your situation, and to get an idea of how he or she would handle it and what costs you could expect. It also gives you the chance to size up the professional and decide whether he or she is pompous or sincere, willing to talk or tight-lipped, comfortable to be with or abrasive—in short, whether this person is right for you.

Talk about Fees

Even if it's difficult for you to talk about money, in the long run it's more difficult not to talk about it—especially if you're hit with unexpected bills. The best time to bring the subject up is right at the start, during the consultation.

Your lawyer or accountant may bill by the hour or charge a flat fee, an open retainer, or (with respect to the lawyer only) a contingency fee. Professionals who bill by the hour set an hourly rate for the value of their services and then charge you according to the amount of time they spend on your case. The major drawback of this system is that you don't know how much your case will cost until it's over.

Professionals charging flat fees tell you in advance the cost of their services, no matter how much time they spend on your case. If it's a straightforward matter and takes very little time, this system can work against you, since flat fees are generally set high.

A far more sensible approach to fees, and the one used by most lawyers and almost all accountants, is the open retainer. Under this system, you pay an initial fee, which it is believed will cover the total cost of services under ordinary circumstances. If something extraordinary happens, you will be asked to pay extra charges based upon the hourly rate.

Contingency fees are paid only to lawyers where litigation is involved. You pay only if you win your case. A lawyer who takes your case on a contingency basis receives a substantial percentage (usually one-third) of the money the court awards you. If you lose your case, your lawyer also loses and gets nothing for his or her time. Because of this risk, contingency fees are used mostly in negligence cases.

Ask for a Retainer Letter

Once you decide who is right for you, ask for a retainer letter. This letter should list the services that he or she will and will not perform. It should specify the fee as well as any extra costs (charges for making long-distance telephone calls and duplicating materials, for instance) that you'll have to pay. If any service you have in mind is not included in your retainer letter, ask about it.

Talk to Your Professional in Writing

Writing a letter is slower than picking up the phone, but it's often the most effective way to communicate. Whenever you think of an important detail that doesn't need your lawyer's immediate attention, put it in writing. Your letter will become part of your permanent file—a telephone call will not. In addition, with respect to a litigation, it's a good idea to keep a diary of your case. As soon as you realize that you have a legal problem on your hands, record any relevant incident, conversation, or expense. Your lawyer can use this documentation as the basis for your case.

Take Notes

Talking to your lawyer or accountant can mean a barrage of facts, dates, figures, and legal advice. With so much happening at once, it's easy to forget an important detail unless you take notes.

Demand Plain English

Jargon is a poor excuse for communication. Tell the professional that you want him or her to use language you can understand.

Talk to the Secretary or Assistant

Take your questions about schedules, mailings, and other nontechnical matters to the office secretary or assistant rather than to the professional. You'll probably get the information you need more quickly this way.

Don't Hold Back Information

It is important to tell all the details of your situation—even those you think are small or insignificant. Holding back information can only work against you.

Don't Tell the Professional How to Do His or Her Work

You hired this person because he or she understands legal rulings or tax laws and can apply them to your situation. Keep in mind that no matter how similar your case may seem to those you may read about, no two cases are alike.

Don't Call All the Time

Lawyers and accountants, like most people, don't like to be nagged. If you waste their time on unimportant phone calls, you'll have trouble getting through when you need to. If your question concerns something that can wait, put it in a letter.

Don't Let a Lawyer or Accountant Make Patronizing or Sexist Remarks

Unfortunately, many male professionals have a tendency to talk down to their female clients, treating them as daughters or wives instead of as independent adults. If you are a woman and come up against this situation, the best way to handle it is head-on. Don't be afraid to get angry if you are called "dear," or told "not to worry your pretty little head." By saying what you think, you'll not only get the respect you deserve, you'll almost certainly get better legal service. And, if your professional is a woman, don't treat her as your alter ego or best friend. Keep the relationship on a professional level.

Don't Be Afraid to Shop Around for a Second Opinion

To get a second opinion, simply tell another lawyer or accountant that you want him or her to review your case. A lawyer will read significant documents, unravel the proceedings for you, explain what has taken place and may also tell you what steps he or she would take next. An accountant will review your tax returns, see how your books are set up, and speak with you regarding your financial situation. It's then up to you to weigh the facts and make a decision. The charge for this service varies, depending on your case and on the professional you choose for the second opinion; be prepared to pay about the same amount as you would for a consultation. Telling your original professional about the second opinion is up to you. If you choose not to, you can be sure that the second-opinion professional will keep the information confidential.

All of the above applies to both lawyers and accountants. But to get a personal view on the practice of accounting, as I have on the practice of law, I interviewed Brian Pecker, CPA, the managing partner of Shine & Company, and Ira Kallem, CPA, the senior partner of the same firm. As accountants who cater largely to people who showed great potential and are "self-made," they were particularly sensitive to the issue of the client being taken seriously.

They wanted you to know that accounting is a business as well as a profession; that a large variety of business opportunities are presented to your accountant, who can in turn introduce you to new opportunities. Their best advice was to choose an accounting firm that not only knew the numbers (which we assume without question) but that was also catering to businesses that you are particularly interested or involved in. Perhaps if you are a manufacturer you're interested in an accounting firm that deals with the retail side of your business or the sales side. Who are their other clients? What is their expertise? Merely by asking these questions, you indicate to an accountant that you are in for the long haul; that you plan to be successful and that you are going to become an important client in the future.

Pecker and Kallem bluntly stated that no one gets rich preparing tax returns and, therefore, accountants who are merely preparers are not enough for you. A time will come in your first fifteen years of working when you must look beyond the mere preparation of the return. You must consider your own business. You must even consider sources of clients that you need and you must consider a firm that has some expertise in real estate and banking. Accounting firms can help you make these associations, as can law firms with bankers, brokers, and other support professionals.

If you are not an entrepreneur but an executive-to-be, focus on a firm that deals in tax planning and investment needs. You don't need contacts from them, you need creativity. "Don't," says Shine & Co., "use the tax moonlighter, the storefront people, or your father-in-law." Find someone who's interested in measuring and meeting your long-term goals.

If you earn $18,000 a year, that's not too little to start thinking big. Speak to people who can give you referrals and get into a network of professionals who'll respect you. Managing partner Brian Pecker affirms that a brand-new client who is young without much money must make a pitch. Sit down and tell the accountant that you want to talk to him or her about your plans. Let them know what your secrets are and your goals.

Rates in accounting firms are generally lower than that of

law firms. A senior partner may earn $100 an hour, as opposed to $250 in a law firm. But in both cases prices are based on the time you have taken and that should never be forgotten.

BANKERS

When it comes to choosing a banker, it is probably the bank that's more important. Banks have varying rules and regulations with respect to their personnel. There are also private banking units within the individual banks. For high-ticket depositors, a banker may be available more frequently and on a more personal basis. In the early years of establishing a relationship, you are interested in a bank that is willing to extend credit to you, is convenient, and has a reasonable policy with regard to checking account charges and interest rate programs. Later on you will also be interested in a bank that renders a great deal of service and services. Can the bank set up a pension plan for you? Does it have a broker-dealer's license, so that it can offer discount brokerage fee transactions if you wish to buy and sell stocks or bonds? Does it have a trust and estates department that can work with your attorney to help plan your eventual estate? Does it have student loan programs for your children or, in the early years, for yourself? Does it have an SBLI program (does it sell life insurance in small quantities, usually up to $30,000 death benefit, at very low rates)?

Beyond these kinds of direct financial services, many banks today are competing in other ways. Some are opening up terminals for check cashing right in major corporate headquarters, so that people can cash their payroll checks before leaving for home on a Friday afternoon. Others have cash depots at which you can withdraw money, using a card, twenty-four hours a day in various locations throughout the area. Other banks are competing not only on the basis of convenience, but also on the basis of information. Branches of some banks give lectures, books, and material on legal matters and other nonexclusively banking subjects. The point is good will, and it can often be a good adjunct to your financial education.

The final line must be convenience for you and willingness of the bank to work with you on various matters.

BROKERS

For the most part, if you are establishing a brand-new account, you are best off if you know or have been recommended to a stockbroker. If you go into any of the major brokerage houses without having a contact to request, you will receive the so-called "man of the day" to help you. This is usually one of the younger and less experienced brokers, who are given a rotating schedule to receive new clients. These assignments are meant to bolster a clientele for them, and they are part of their arrangement with the brokerage house at which they work. Because they are "hungry," these less experienced professionals may give you the best service and the most respect you could marshall. However, in dealing with them it is important that you be much more knowledgeable and experienced than you would need to be with a more established broker.

If you know what you want to buy, a stockbroker can become nothing more than an order taker. No advice is necessary, therefore if this is the case there is no reason to pay for any in the form of large commissions. If you are well informed and do not need any special services, a discount brokerage house is the answer for you. They advertise freely on radio and in the financial publications. Each will send you a rate schedule and they are very competitive with respect to pricing. Your bank may also have established a broker-dealer department. If so, they usually charge slightly above the discount brokerage rates but also give no services. You might like the convenience of using the bank; then again, you might like the phone-in procedures of the discount brokerage houses, which often allow you to open an account and place an order by phone rather than in person. Check these out.

Stockbrokers (I am one) must take a licensing exam. These are given by the NASD (National Association of Securities Dealers). The exam is very difficult and even the youngest broker should be respected for passing the test. Other than the examination, it is impossible to tell what exactly your broker's background is without actually asking. In fact, because of the usual method of structuring a brokerage office, your broker may not have an office of his or her own and may not even have a wall on which to hang diplomas. So ask about this background.

A broker will generally follow a particular industry or a certain group of industries, or certain select stocks. In their own way, brokers specialize. This is largely to do with the kind of research favored by their brokerage house. Ask whether they specialize in options, if that's what's interesting to you. Are they fully familiar with income-producing investments? Also, when discussing fees and commissions with brokers, remember that sometimes there are magic words. For example, when you buy a stock you will pay a commission; however if you buy a bond, you may pay a mark-up. The amount of commission will not be readily apparent to you unless you ask what the mark-up is on a bond. A normal mark-up is anywhere between $5 to $10 per thousand-dollar purchase.

If your broker is selling you a mutual fund, there might be no commission in it for him or her—these are the no-load funds we discussed in Chapter 3. Load funds are charged in a variety of different ways: sometimes commission is paid from your up-front purchase price; other times, commissions are staged in and the management company pays the broker instead, provided you hold your interest in the mutual fund over a period of three to five years and they make their money back in yearly management fees. Ask your broker how he or she is compensated for anything you buy. Brokers can sell certificates of deposit, gold stocks, and much more. An open discussion of compensation is usually the best method of approach.

All brokers are allowed to give discounts. A broker who's a big producer for his firm (sells a lot) can often give up to 40 percent of the commissions back to the customer if he or she believes that this customer is worthwhile to court. You probably won't get such thrilling discounts at the beginning—however, you never know. Always ask about discounted commissions.

You have learned many rules and many truths, and perhaps many of your cherished beliefs have been debunked. Now that you have learned the rules, try them out, get used to them, have a plan, and then go ahead and *break them* every once in a while. It is not that you cannot be creative during your wealth-building years. It is just that, like Picasso, you must learn to draw before you can become an artistic genius.

Good luck!

Index

About the Author

Adriane G. Berg, an attorney and financial planner, is the author also of *How to Stop Fighting About Money & Make Some*, *Moneythink*, and *Your Kids, Your Money*. A graduate of New York University Law School, where she was editor of the Law Review, she is a former member of the Board of Directors of the New York Chapter of the International Association for Financial Planning and currently serves as chair of the New York State Bar Association in Estate Planning. She teaches at the New School for Social Research, conducts financial planning seminars for individuals, professional groups, and corporations, and appears frequently on radio and television. She lives in New York City.

Adriane Berg's Personal Finance and Money Management Books from Newmarket Press

HOW TO STOP FIGHTING ABOUT MONEY & MAKE SOME
A Couple's Guide to Financial Success

Attorney, estate planner, and Financial News Network commentator, Adriane Berg shows couples of all ages and incomes how to take money matters "out of the bedroom and into the boardroom," and begin making money as a team. Her practical approach includes a valuable 10-step home money management program that covers recordkeeping, budgeting, investment decisions, and much more. "A no-nonsense guide to help couples get beyond their financial problems and start making money decisions that will work for them."—*Philadelphia Inquirer*. 256 pages.

YOUR WEALTH-BUILDING YEARS
Financial Planning for 18- to 38-Year-Olds
Second Edition

This invaluable handbook for young adults shows how they can take advantage of their biggest asset—time—and take control of their financial destiny. Berg explains real estate, job benefits, financial instruments, and budgeting in addition to shared housing and socially responsible investing, both growing concerns of young investors. "Entertaining and informative …An excellent primer and reference tool."—*Nashville Banner*. "First rate."—*Publishers Weekly*. 272 pages.

Order from your local bookstore or write to:
NEWMARKET PRESS, 18 East 48th Street, New York, N.Y. 10017
Please send me:
_____ copies of HOW TO STOP FIGHTING ABOUT MONEY & MAKE SOME @ $18.95 (hardcover)
_____ copies of YOUR WEALTH-BUILDING YEARS: Financial Planning for 18- to 38-Year-Olds @ $10.95 (trade paperback)

For postage and handling, add $2.00 for the first book, plus $1.00 for each additional book. Allow 4-6 weeks for delivery. Prices and availability are subject to change.

I enclose check or money order payable to NEWMARKET PRESS in the amount of $ _____ .

NAME _____

ADDRESS _____

CITY/STATE/ZIP _____

For quotes on quantity purchases, or for a copy of our catalog, please write Newmarket Press, 18 East 48th Street, New York, N.Y. 10017, or call the Sales Department at (212) 832-3575.

BOBBERG 4/90